INTRODUCING
ISSUES WITH
OPPOSING
VIEWPOINTS®

Cheating

Other books in the Introducing Issues
with Opposing Viewpoints series:

AIDS
Civil Liberties
Cloning
The Death Penalty
Gangs
Gay Marriage
Genetic Engineering
Smoking
Terrorism

INTRODUCING
ISSUES WITH
OPPOSING
VIEWPOINTS®

Cheating

Patty Jo Sawvel, *Book Editor*

Christine Nasso, *Publisher*
Elizabeth Des Chenes, *Managing Editor*

GREENHAVEN PRESS
A part of Gale, Cengage Learning

GALE
CENGAGE Learning

Detroit • New York • San Francisco • New Haven, Conn • Waterville, Maine • London

GALE
CENGAGE Learning

© 2008 Gale, a part of Cengage Learning

For more information, contact
Greenhaven Press
27500 Drake Rd.
Farmington Hills, MI 48331-3535
Or you can visit our Internet site at gale.cengage.com

LIBRARY OF CONGRESS CATALOGING-IN-PUBLICATION DATA

Cheating / Patty Jo Sawvel, book editor.
   p. cm. — (Introducing issues with opposing viewpoints)
  Includes bibliographical references and index.
  ISBN-13: 978-0-7377-3802-5 (hardcover)
  1. Honesty—Juvenile literature. 2. Cheating (Education)—Juvenile literature. I. Sawvel, Patty Jo, 1958-
  BJ1533.H7C446 2008
  179'.8—dc22

                         2007037106

ISBN-10: 0-7377-3802-2 (hardcover)

Printed in the United States of America
3 4 5 6 7 12 11 10 09 08

Contents

Foreword

Indulging in a wide spectrum of ideas, beliefs, and perspectives is a critical cornerstone of democracy. After all, it is often debates over differences of opinion, such as whether to legalize abortion, how to treat prisoners, or when to enact the death penalty that shape our society and drive it forward. Such diversity of thought is frequently regarded as the hallmark of a healthy and civilized culture. As the Reverend Clifford Schutjer of the First Congregational Church in Mansfield, Ohio, declared in a 2001 sermon, "Surrounding oneself with only like-minded people, restricting what we listen to or read only to what we find agreeable is irresponsible. Refusing to entertain doubts once we make up our minds is a subtle but deadly form of arrogance." With this advice in mind, Introducing Issues with Opposing Viewpoints books aim to open readers' minds to the critically divergent views that comprise our world's most important debates.

Introducing Issues with Opposing Viewpoints simplifies for students the enormous and often overwhelming mass of material now available via print and electronic media. Collected in every volume is an array of opinions that capture the essence of a particular controversy or topic. Introducing Issues with Opposing Viewpoints books embody the spirit of nineteenth-century journalist Charles A. Dana's axiom: "Fight for your opinions, but do not believe that they contain the whole truth, or the only truth." Absorbing such contrasting opinions teaches students to analyze the strength of an argument and compare it to its opposition. From this process readers can inform and strengthen their own opinions, or be exposed to new information that will change their minds. Introducing Issues with Opposing Viewpoints is a mosaic of different voices. The authors are statesmen, pundits, academics, journalists, corporations, and ordinary people who have felt compelled to share their experiences and ideas in a public forum. Their words have been collected from newspapers, journals, books, speeches, interviews, and the Internet, the fastest growing body of opinionated material in the world.

Introducing Issues with Opposing Viewpoints shares many of the well-known features of its critically acclaimed parent series, Opposing Viewpoints. The articles are presented in a pro/con format, allowing readers to absorb divergent perspectives side by side. Active reading questions preface each viewpoint, requiring the student to approach the material thoughtfully and carefully. Useful charts, graphs, and cartoons supplement each article. A thorough introduction provides readers with crucial background on an issue. An annotated bibliography points the reader toward articles, books, and Web sites that contain additional information on the topic. An appendix of organizations to contact contains a wide variety of charities, nonprofit organizations, political groups, and private enterprises that each hold a position on the issue at hand. Finally, a comprehensive index allows readers to locate content quickly and efficiently.

Introducing Issues with Opposing Viewpoints is also significantly different from Opposing Viewpoints. As the series title implies, its presentation will help introduce students to the concept of opposing viewpoints, and learn to use this material to aid in critical writing and debate. The series' four-color, accessible format makes the books attractive and inviting to readers of all levels. In addition, each viewpoint has been carefully edited to maximize a reader's understanding of the content. Short but thorough viewpoints capture the essence of an argument. A substantial, thought-provoking essay question placed at the end of each viewpoint asks the student to further investigate the issues raised in the viewpoint, compare and contrast two authors' arguments, or consider how one might go about forming an opinion on the topic at hand. Each viewpoint contains sidebars that include at-a-glance information and handy statistics. A Facts About section located in the back of the book further supplies students with relevant facts and figures.

Following in the tradition of the Opposing Viewpoints series, Greenhaven Press continues to provide readers with invaluable exposure to the controversial issues that shape our world. As John Stuart Mill once wrote: "The only way in which a human being can make some approach to knowing the whole of a subject is by hearing what can be said about it by persons of every variety of opinion and studying all modes in which it can be looked at by every character of mind. No wise man ever acquired his wisdom in any mode but this." It is to this principle that Introducing Issues with Opposing Viewpoints books are dedicated.

Introduction

"One of the most important changes needed to reduce cheating in many places is to banish the perception that 'everybody does it.'"

David Callahan, author of *The Cheating Culture: Why More Americans Are Doing Wrong to Get Ahead.*

In 2006 the Josephson Institute of Ethics announced that of 36,122 high school students surveyed, 60 percent admitted to cheating on a test and 33 percent plagiarized by copying an Internet document. As 17-year-old Alice Newhall, explained in a CNN special report on cheating, "Cheating is a shortcut and a pretty efficient one in a lot of cases."

Handheld technology has made cheating even easier. *The Real News* in Missouri quoted an anonymous high school student who said, "I recorded an essay on my iPod at home, and it was supposed to only be in-class preparation. While I was writing the essay, I listened to what I wrote at home. I titled the track a Pink Floyd song." He added, "Man, that was a great way to cheat."

Across the nation, teachers have reported students using MP3 players, cell phones, graphing calculators, Zunes, BlackBerry® devices, and other handheld technology to store and access unauthorized information or to access the Internet during tests. At first glance, it may seem that handheld devices are to blame for increased student cheating. However, many students have an opposing viewpoint.

Donald McCabe, the founding president of the Center for Academic Integrity, polled students to find out why they cheated. It wasn't because cheating was easy. Next to academic pressure, students cited the poor example the adult world is setting. "They (students) don't understand why they should be held to a higher standard," McCabe said.

Newell believes that the current culture in America rewards cheating behavior. She said, "What's important is to get ahead. And, if you learn to cut corners to do that, you're going to be saving yourself time and energy. In the real world, that's what's going on." Newspapers routinely expose "real world" incidents of corporate fraud, tax cheating, and sports doping—all of which give cheaters an advantage over their competitors.

Students find evidence of adult cheating right within the public education system. In recent years, schools in several states, including Illinois, New Jersey, Ohio, and Texas made headline news when teachers and administrators changed students' answers on state mandated tests to improve their schools' test scores. Perhaps more telling than the cheating itself, is what happens to teachers after they are fired. According to a 2006 story in *The Dallas Morning Star,* reporting on a local incident, most teachers were able to find new jobs within weeks. Many are working in schools adjacent to their former schools.[1]

Coming down to the classroom level, the culture in each individual classroom has a significant impact on the amount of cheating that will take place within the class. According to McCabe, student cheating is more prevalent when teachers ignore the offenses or treat them too lightly. McCabe documented this phenomena in the paper, "It Takes a Village: Academic Dishonesty," where he noted, "If students see others cheating and the faculty who fail to see it or choose to ignore it, they are likely to conclude that cheating is necessary to remain competitive. Many students ask, 'If faculty members aren't concerned, why should I be?'"

Though McCabe was referring to the college classroom, reports indicate that the same culture exists in K-12 classrooms. In a newspaper interview, Jennifer Salaz, a Spanish teacher, said she ignores student cheating on her daily five-minute quizzes. "If I was going to worry about everyone cheating on these, I would go insane," Salaz said. Instead, she focuses on things that are more important, such as in-class presentations. Her fellow teacher, Joe Matteson, who teaches biology, said that it didn't matter if students copied each other's homework. However, he monitors students very closely during tests.

Similarly, students seem to be adopting their own standards for cheating. For many students, cheating on homework is not a big deal, but they draw the line at cheating on a test. For other students, the line is more blurry. After a California high school student was caught

[1] Joshua Benton, "Cheating Hasn't Hurt Wilmer-Hutchins Teachers: Exclusive: Accused W-HISD Educators Hired in Other Schools," *Dallas Morning Star*, October 1, 2006.

studying a stolen copy of the advanced placement history test, he told the local newspaper, "I don't consider it an extreme form of cheating." He was expelled, as was his friend who stole a paper copy of the test. Within 48 hours of the incident, school officials surveyed classmates about the theft. Under the protection of anonymity, students wrote of widespread cheating. Two incidents involved students breaking into their teacher's computer files. While these two students used new technology, they did not use handheld devices.

A 2007 survey of high school students in New Mexico had similar findings. Less than six percent of cheating students used handheld technology to cheat. The vast majority said "they borrowed others' homework or glanced on neighbors' tests to perform better." Because most cheating is still done the "old fashioned" way, students are upset when their iPods, cell phones, MP3 players or other handheld technology devices are either banned or confiscated at school in an effort to reduce student cheating.[2]

In May of 2007, thirteen-year-old Adena Lin wrote to the *Toronto Star,* "New York City, Seattle, and a high school in Ontario have already banned music players. Will Toronto follow in their footsteps? Let's hope not. I mean, isn't taking away our cell phones enough? I don't think it will solve the cheating problem. And what about those who don't cheat, but suffer under the ban as well? That's very unfair."

Handheld technology and its impact on student cheating illustrates the importance of examining opposing viewpoints on issues that affect the level of personal choice and freedom that people enjoy in society. The role of new technology in both promoting and protecting against cheating is just one of the issues explored by authors in this anthology. *Introducing Issues with Opposing Viewpoints: Cheating* offers an examination of cheating throughout society—whether it be in schools, business, or within relationships.

[2] Brandon Garcia, "Majority of Students Not Cheating with New Technology," *Santa Fe New Mexican,* February 25, 2007.

Chapter 1

Do Americans Live in a Cheating Culture?

Hand-held technology has made it much more possible for students to cheat in class.

Some Schoolteachers Cheat

Steven D. Levitt and Stephen J. Dubner

"High-stakes testing has so radically changed the incentives for teachers that they now have added reason to cheat."

In this viewpoint, author and economist Steven Levitt explains how schoolteachers were caught cheating in the Chicago Public Schools. He recounts that teacher cheating spiked in 1996, the year that "high stakes" testing dramatically changed teachers' incentives. Economist Stephen D. Levitt was awarded the John Bates Clark Medal honoring him as the best American economist under forty. He joined Stephen J. Dubner, a national best-selling author and writer for the *New York Times* and *the New Yorker*, to coauthor the book *Freakonomics*, from which this viewpoint was taken.

AS YOU READ, CONSIDER THE FOLLOWING QUESTIONS:

1. According to the author, why does "high stakes" testing give teachers reason to cheat?
2. According to the author, how much teacher cheating was revealed when the Chicago data was analyzed?

3. In the author's opinion, why was a control group needed for the retest?

The most volatile current debate among American school administrators, teachers, parents, and students concerns "high-stakes" testing. The stakes are considered high because instead of simply testing students to measure their progress, schools are increasingly held accountable for the results. The federal government mandated high-stakes testing as part of the No Child Left Behind law, signed by President [George W.] Bush in 2002. . . .

The Chicago Public School system embraced high-stakes testing in 1996. . . . In order to be promoted, every student in third, sixth, and eighth grade had to manage a minimum score on the standardized, multiple-choice exam known as the Iowa Test of Basic Skills. . . .

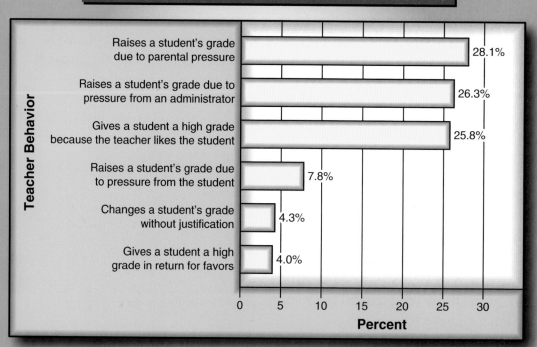

Percentage of Educators Agreeing That the Following Unethical Behavior by K-12 Teachers Occurs Frequently

Teacher Behavior:
- Raises a student's grade due to parental pressure — 28.1%
- Raises a student's grade due to pressure from an administrator — 26.3%
- Gives a student a high grade because the teacher likes the student — 25.8%
- Raises a student's grade due to pressure from the student — 7.8%
- Changes a student's grade without justification — 4.3%
- Gives a student a high grade in return for favors — 4.0%

Percent

Taken from: The Journal of Psychology, 2006.

Teachers Have Reason to Cheat

High-stakes testing has so radically changed the incentives for teachers that they . . . now have added reason to cheat. With high-stakes testing, a teacher whose students test poorly can be censured or passed over for a raise or promotion. If the entire school does poorly, federal funding can be withheld; if the school is put on probation, the teacher stands to be fired. High-stakes testing also present teachers with some positive incentives. If her students do well enough, she might find herself praised, promoted, and even richer: the state of California at one point introduced bonuses of $25,000 for teachers who produced big test-score gains.

And if a teacher were to survey this newly incentivized landscape and consider somehow inflating her students' scores, she just might be persuaded by one final incentive: teacher cheating is rarely looked for, hardly ever detected, and just about never punished.

There Are Many Ways to Cheat

How might a teacher go about cheating? There are any number of possibilities, from the brazen to the sophisticated. A fifth-grade student in Oakland recently came home from school and gaily told her mother that her super-nice teacher had written the answers to the state exam right there on the chalkboard. . . . (The Oakland teacher was duly fired.) There are more subtle ways to inflate students' scores. A teacher can simply give students extra time to complete the test. If she obtains a copy of the exam early—that is, illegitimately—she can prepare them for specific questions. More broadly, she can "teach to the test," basing her lesson plans on questions from past years' exams, which isn't considered cheating but certainly violates the spirit of the test.

Since these tests all have multiple-choice answers, with no penalty for wrong guesses, a teacher might instruct her students to randomly fill in every blank as the clock is winding down, perhaps inserting a long string of Bs or an alternating pattern of Bs and Cs. She might even fill in the blanks for them after they've left the room.

> **FAST FACT**
>
> In 2007, there was evidence of more than 50,000 cases of cheating in Texas on the Texas Assessment of Knowledge and Skills test (TAKS).

But if a teacher *really* wanted to cheat—and make it worth her while—she might collect her students' answer sheets and, in the hour or so before turning them in to be read by an electronic scanner, erase the wrong answers and fill in correct ones. . . .

Cheating Can Be Detected

The Chicago Public School system made available a database of the test answers for every CPS student from third grade through seventh grade from 1993 to 2000. This amounts to roughly 30,000 students per grade per year, more than 700,000 sets of test answers, and nearly 100 million individual answers. The data, organized by classroom, included each student's question-by-question answer strings for reading and math tests. . . . The data also included some information

Teachers are under close scrutiny on how they prepare their students for tests.

about each teacher and demographic information for every student, as well as his or her past and future test scores—which would prove a key element in detecting the teacher cheating.

Now it was time to construct an algorithm [a mathematical procedure] that could tease some conclusions from this mass of data. . . .

An analysis of the entire Chicago data reveals evidence of teacher cheating in more than two hundred classrooms per year, roughly 5 percent of the total. This is a conservative estimate, since the algorithm was able to identify only the most egregious form of cheating—in which teachers systematically changed students' answer—and not the many subtler ways a teacher might cheat. In a recent study among North Carolina schoolteachers, some 35 percent of the respondents said they had witnessed their colleagues cheating in some fashion, whether by giving students extra time, suggesting answers, or manually changing students' answers. . . .

Cheating Can Be Confirmed

In early 2002, the new CEO of the Chicago Public Schools, Arne Duncan, contacted the study's authors. . . . He wanted to make sure that the teachers identified by the algorithm as cheaters were truly cheating—and then do something about it. . . .

Duncan . . . decided to readminister the standardized exam. To make the retest results convincing, some non-cheaters were needed as a control group. The best control group? The classrooms shown by the algorithm to have the best teachers, in which big gains were thought to have been legitimately attained. If those classrooms held their gains while the classrooms with a suspected cheater lost ground, the cheating teachers could hardly argue that their students did worse only because the scores wouldn't count. . . .

The retest was given a few weeks after the original exam. The children were not told the reason for the retest. Neither were the teachers. But they may have gotten the idea when it was announced that CPS officials, not the teachers, would administer the test. The teachers were asked to stay in the classroom with their students, but they would not be allowed to even touch the answer sheets.

The results were as compelling as the cheating algorithm had predicted. In the classrooms chosen as controls, where no cheating was suspected, scores stayed about the same or even rose. In contrast, the students with the teachers identified as cheaters scored far worse, by an average of more than a full grade level.

As a result, the Chicago Public School system began to fire its cheating teachers. The evidence was only strong enough to get rid of a dozen of them, but the many other cheaters had been duly warned. The final outcome of the Chicago study is further testament to the power of incentives: the following year, cheating by teachers fell more than 30 percent.

EVALUATING THE AUTHORS' ARGUMENTS:

In this viewpoint, authors Steven Levitt and Stephen Dubner proved that high positive incentives (promotions or pay raises) and high negative incentives (censures or firing) caused more teachers to cheat. Other teachers with the identical incentives remained honest. In your opinion, what is the deciding factor or motive involved when a teacher chooses to cheat? Does cheating by a teacher harm the students? Please give reasons for your answers.

Most Schoolteachers Are Honest

Duncan McInnes

"The large majority of teachers do not cheat in regards to 'high stakes' tests or student's grades."

In this viewpoint, the author states that while the vast majority of teachers do not cheat, many have unfair roadblocks placed in their paths. Using the real-life experience of a first-year teacher, Mr. Nacnud (name changed to protect his identity), the author itemizes unfair roadblocks. On more than one occasion, this teacher was advised to cheat to overcome a roadblock, but refused. Duncan McInnes is an award-winning sports and news editor and a columnist for the *Kernersville News*, from which this viewpoint was taken.

AS YOU READ, CONSIDER THE FOLLOWING QUESTIONS:
1. According to this viewpoint, at most public high schools, how are first year teachers treated?
2. According to the author, in the class of 35 students, what happened to four male students and three female students?
3. According to this viewpoint, during the last three months of the year, what was the primary directive for Mr. Nacnud?

I n recent years, overworked and underappreciated teachers have received another ultimatum in the form of "high stakes" or "accountability testing" spawned by the No Child Left Behind program. In many respects, the stakes for "high stakes testing" are far higher for the teachers and the administrators than for the students themselves. In many school systems, how much money a school may receive is based on how the students perform on "high stakes" tests. In every school in the nation, teachers are meticulously judged and evaluated by how well their students perform on the "high stakes" tests and by the overall grades students receive.

Most Teachers Do Not Cheat

The large majority of teachers do not cheat in regards to "high stakes" tests or student's grades. It could be argued however, that with all that is at stake it is surprising that more teachers don't bend the rules when faced with possibly losing their job or school funding due to the results of No Child Left Behind and end-of-course test results.

Challenges for new teachers test their morals and encourage cheating to over come obstacles put up by school administrators.

While some aspects of teaching have changed dramatically in the past 15 years or so, some truisms remain. At most public high schools, first year teachers are sometimes treated with less respect from their peers and administrators than the students themselves.

A good friend of mine (in order to protect the innocent, or guilty depending upon your point of view, I'll call him Mac Nacnud) provided a depressing, but unfortunately not atypical account of what his first year of teaching was like.

Teachers Want To Help

Mr. Nacnud entered his first year of teaching with the same mindset as most first year teachers. He wanted to help mold the minds of today's youth in a positive manner, help them to read and write more proficiently and, in general, become people who would eventually benefit society as a whole.

Nacnud found that several students, all of which were major disciplinary problems, had originally been on other teacher's class lists but had been transferred to his classes literally days before school officially started. Some older tenured teachers did apologize for their actions, and explained their reasoning with "I just could not handle dealing with that kid for another year."

After one week of attempting to teach his large second period Basic . . . English class, Nacnud asked, "What the hell is wrong with these kids?"

Some Students Have Special Needs

It turns out 12 of the 27 students in the class were classified as LD (Learning Difficulty) or special needs kids. No one had bothered to inform him of this and he had received no learning difficulty or special needs training in any of his education classes. One of the kids was legally deaf. Eventually, after talking to the administration, a special education teacher was assigned to help with the class.

Surprisingly, the second period class was far better than the fifth period Basic English class.

This class had 35 students. By the end of the year, four of the male students in this class had been arrested for assault and three of the female students got pregnant. On the last day of school, only 17 students were left in the class and only nine students attended class enough and/or scored well enough on tests to pass Basic English. One of the students left in the class at the end of the year had been caught smoking crack in the bathroom by Mr. Nacnud. No disciplinary action was taken by the administration and he was back in class the next day.

The pass/fail rate was far higher for the second period class, which goes to show that the desire to learn may be more important than the aptitude to learn.

Teachers Get Bad Advice

Mr. Nacnud was advised by some teachers to cheat in regards to student's grades. Grades were based on the seven, not the ten-point scale. But Nacnud was advised to pass kids whose grades were 58, 47 and 42 respectively. He did not.

There were more than a few road bumps on the first year teaching road for Mr. Nacnud. In the second week of school, the best player on his JV soccer team died in a car accident. In the second semester of school, a student in his second period class died from what was deemed a heart attack.

> **FAST FACT**
>
> According to a study conducted by the Education Policy Research Institute, increases in high-stakes testing are related to larger numbers of student drop-outs.

The good folks at Central office decided the best day to do their evaluation of Nacnud's teaching abilities with his second period class was the day after his student died from a cocaine overdose. Needless to say, the students had things other than education on their minds. Mr. Nacnud was also an assistant varsity and head JV coach for both the women's and men's soccer teams and by forced conscription was made the teacher representative for three non-academic clubs.

Some Teach to the Test

During the last three months of the school year, the primary directive ordered by the administration was for Mr. Nacnud to do everything possible to ensure his students, many of whom were at a reading level far below the grade they were in, could pass the end of course test. In

Teachers Rate #2 as Most Trusted Professionals

Honesty and Ethics Ratings by Profession

1. Nurses
2. **Grade school teachers**
3. Pharmacists
4. Military officers
5. Medical doctors
6. Officers
7. Clergy
8. Judges
9. Day care providers
10. Bankers

Taken from: Gallup Poll, Honesty and Ethical Standards of Professions Survey, 2004.

a very general sense, you could say he was "teaching the test," but he did this in a way that went along with the original curriculum. The most successful "teaching the test" project was getting inner city kids to understand "The Iliad." All this required was rewriting "The Iliad" in contemporary language they could relate to and allowing them to act out parts of the epic in class.

In the end, more of the students in his second and fifth period English class than expected passed the end of course test, but the pass/fail ratio was below the national average. This was of course all Mr. Nacnud's fault. He should have been able to get students that read at a less than sixth grade reading level to pass a tenth grade end of course English test.

Teachers Cannot Take All the Blame
Across the nation, thousands of English teachers are having many of

the same problems Mr. Nacnud had in his one year of teaching. All of these teachers are held accountable when students that can barely write a sentence and students that are in the English as a Second Language program can't meet the demands of the No Child Left Behind program and other standardized tests.

In the minds of the brain trust behind the No Child Left Behind program, kids don't fail and parents are never at fault. It's only the teachers that can fail, and school systems still stupidly complain about why there is a teacher shortage.

EVALUATING THE AUTHOR'S ARGUMENTS:

According to the author, Mr. Nacnud was cheated by the school system when several students with major disciplinary problems were transferred into his class, instead of remaining dispersed among many teachers. Using Mr. Nacnud's experience and what you learned in the previous viewpoint about "high stakes" testing—whose fault might it be if a student, a classroom, or even a school does poorly on high stakes tests? Give reasons for your answers.

Taxpayers Cheat the Government

Saul Shapiro

"One scam alone accounted for $2 billion of faked losses and about $300 million in uncollected taxes."

According to this viewpoint, the Senate Homeland Security and Governmental Affairs Subcommittees on Investigations estimates that millionaires, billionaires, and corporations cheat the government out of as much as $100 billion in taxes each year. The author explains that one popular scam involves phony offshore companies that generate fake losses. These fake losses are then used to shelter real gains from taxation. This tax cheating costs honest taxpayers about $70 billion each year. Saul Shapiro, author of this editorial, is editor of the Waterloo-Cedar Falls *Courier* in Iowa, from which this viewpoint was taken.

AS YOU READ, CONSIDER THE FOLLOWING QUESTIONS:
1. According to this viewpoint, how did one of the leading purveyors of illegal tax ploys cheat the government out of billions of tax dollars?
2. In this viewpoint, how did Senator Carl Levin describe the faked losses and uncollected taxes?
3. According to this editorial, the Senate subcommittee report is urging what changes to stop tax cheating?

Saul Shapiro, "Taxpayers Foot Bill for White-Collar Criminals," *Waterloo-Cedar Falls Courier (Iowa),* August 4, 2006, p. B2. Copyright © 2006 *Waterloo-Cedar Falls Courier (Iowa).* Reproduced by permission.

Accarding to a report released Tuesday by the Senate Homeland Security and Governmental Affairs Subcommittee on Investigations, as much as $100 billion in tax revenue may be lost annually to elaborate scams involving phony offshore corporations set up in countries with little financial oversight. The paper transactions transfer no funds, but purport to show an investment in a company experiencing losses.

The capital gains losses help the investors reduce or eliminate capital gains taxes. The committee estimates U.S. multimillionaires and billionaires have saved an estimated $40 billion to $70 billion in taxes, while corporations have dodged another $30 billion.

The report also stated honest taxpayers pay 7 cents on each tax

Court prosecutions of white-collar tax evaders costs the everyday person millions of dollars in tax money.

dollar—about $70 billion per year—to offset the deviousness of tax cheats.

One Scam Can Cost Billions

One of the leading purveyors of illegal tax ploys was a Seattle-based firm, Quellos LLC, which the committee found used $9.6 billion in "fake securities transactions" to generate "billions of dollars in fake capital losses."

One 1999 Quellos scam was known as POINT—Personal

Optimized Investment Transaction—sold stock in nonexistent companies on the Isle of Man. Reminiscent of Enron's use of phony offshore companies named for "Star Wars" characters, Quellos corporations were anointed with crayon colors. All told, POINT alone accounted for $2 billion of faked losses and about $300 million in uncollected taxes.

Said subcommittee member [Senator] Carl Levin, [Michigan Democrat], "They just wrote down numbers on paper and claimed losses. It was just like fantasy baseball, except the taxes not paid were for real."

The Quellos schemes were overseen by accountant Larry Scheinfeld, who had been formerly employed at the KPMG accounting firm, which has been linked to other illegal tax dodges.

One of Scheinfeld's deals created nonexistent companies on the Isle of Man aimed at sheltering money for Woody Johnson, the owner of the New York Jets and a member of the family that founded the Johnson & Johnson health care company.

Chuck Wilk, a tax lawyer, e-mailed Scheinfeld, "Ain't capitalism great!" Scheinfeld responded, "I just hope that Woody doesn't get cold feet or have the IRS select his return for an audit."

"Mighty Morphin Power Rangers" producer Haim Saban paid Quellos and lawyers $54 million in fees to shelter $300 million in taxes from his interest in the sale of the Family Channel and other properties.

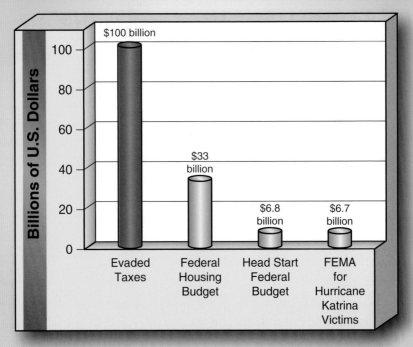

Lost Tax Revenues Could Fund Valuable Programs

$100 billion

$33 billion

$6.8 billion

$6.7 billion

Billions of U.S. Dollars

Evaded Taxes

Federal Housing Budget

Head Start Federal Budget

FEMA for Hurricane Katrina Victims

Taken from: Editorial, "No Haven for Tax Cheats," Boston Globe, August 06, 2006.

Attorney Lewis Steinberg, who wrote an opinion letter supporting the legality of some Quellos tax shelters, was chairman of the American Bar Association's tax section in 2004.

Both Johnson and Saban, characterized by the subcommittee as victims in their quest to shelter taxes, are cooperating with federal prosecutors.

Three years ago the staff of the same Senate subcommittee reported KPMG scams using a series of loans and other transactions to establish large tax losses to offset capital gains.

Last year KPMG admitted "unlawful conduct" in selling tax shelters in a successful attempt to escape a corporate criminal indictment, which had been the undoing of the Arthur Andersen firm in the Enron debacle.

Instead, the tax fraud trial of 16 KPMG partners and two others had been scheduled to begin in July, but has been delayed four months.

Tax Law Changes Are Necessary

The Senate subcommittee report urges changes in the law to lift the veil of secrecy from tax-avoidance schemes and to go after the investment, accounting and law firms that concoct them as well as the banks that facilitate them. And it wants changes in the rules that have made offshore tax havens so attractive.

Congress should take that initiative.

Apparently, the accounting fraud cases involving Enron, WorldCom, Tyco, Adelphia and others didn't strike sufficient fear into the hearts of many white-collar crooks. Given the additional tools, prosecutors need to take them on with a sense of zeal, lest honest taxpayers keep picking up the bill for these cons.

EVALUATING THE AUTHOR'S ARGUMENTS:

In this viewpoint, the author explains how some rich people (tax-avoiders) use phony offshore corporations to cheat the government out of billions of tax dollars. To concoct these "elaborate schemes," the tax-avoiders have to enlist the help of investment, accounting, and law firms. In your opinion, what effect might it have on future tax cheating if the enlisted companies were prosecuted along with the tax-avoiders? Explain your answer.

Most Taxpayers Are Honest

The Wall Street Journal

"Nina Olson, the IRS's taxpayer advocate, told Congress last year that IRS auditors have found an estimated 94% of non-compliance is the result of honest mistakes."

According to this editorial, the Internal Revenue Service (IRS) estimates the current "tax gap" to be about $290 billion each year. This "tax gap" is the difference between what the IRS believes taxpayers owe and what the IRS actually collects. This viewpoint states that most taxpayers—85 percent—pay their taxes honestly. Sometimes taxpayers are audited by the IRS and the IRS finds them to have underpaid their taxes. Ninety-four percent of the time, this is not because the taxpayers are dishonest. It is because taxpayers are confused by the 17,000-page tax-code. Instead of simplifying the tax code, Congress is considering increasing tax regulations and enforcement. According to this editorial, these new measures will increase the burden on the honest majority, while having little impact on the cheating minority. The *Wall Street Journal*, from which this viewpoint was taken, has an average daily circulation of 2 million copies. The editorial page takes a free-market view of economic issues and has been awarded several Pulitzer prizes.

"The Tax Gap 'Myth'," *The Wall Street Journal,* January 30, 2007, p. A16. Copyright © 2007 Dow Jones & Company, Inc. All rights reserved. Reprinted with permission of *The Wall Street Journal.*

To put the tax gap in perspective, consider that the [Internal Revenue Service] (IRS) took in tax receipts in fiscal 2005 of more than $2.2 trillion and that the overall U.S. tax compliance rate is about 85%. This isn't perfect, but it also isn't Italy. It's especially good considering the U.S. tax system is based on voluntary compliance. Nina Olson, the IRS's taxpayer advocate, told Congress last year that IRS auditors have found that an estimated 94% of non-compliance is the result of honest mistakes by tax filers who simply don't understand the 17,000-page beast of a tax code.

FAST FACT

In a national survey commissioned by Bankrate.com 86 percent of respondents said they have never "fudged" the truth on their taxes.

One obvious answer would be to simplify the code (more on that later). But this requires political will, so Congress naturally prefers the easier route of ratcheting up taxpayer regulation and enforcement. One popular solution is to increase dramatically the information taxpayers must report to the IRS.

Paperwork May Increase

Some potential illustrations: Brokers would have to report securities sales information to the IRS, the better to monitor capital gains. Individuals who participate in online auctions such as eBay would have to file a tax form about their transactions. Americans would be required to file expanded mortgage interest forms, while mortgage lenders would have to report loan information. State and local govern-

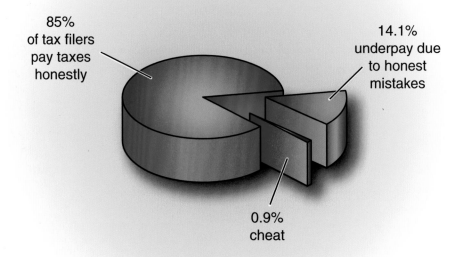

85%
of tax filers
pay taxes
honestly

14.1%
underpay due
to honest
mistakes

0.9%
cheat

Taken from: "The 'Tax Gap' Myth," The Wall Street Journal, January 30, 2007.

ments would have to provide their tax data to Washington, the better to double-check deductions.

Our personal favorite would require that Americans withhold taxes from any cash payments they make to such individual contractors as babysitters, gardeners or plumbers. They'll love that one in the suburbs. Implicit in all these new plans is a much bigger IRS staff to monitor and chase tax miscreants.

Taxes May Increase

Here's another bad idea: Many doctors and lawyers who are incorporated under subchapter S will often pay themselves lower wages but higher dividends, in order to reduce self-employment taxes. The law is vague on the limits of this practice, and it is undoubtedly abused. But the Joint Tax Committee's preferred solution is to make all pro-

IRS Commissioner Mark Everson discusses how to reduce the tax gap during Senate hearings.

fessional income—even dividend payments—subject to self-employment taxes; this is nothing more than a backdoor tax hike.

All voluntary tax compliance systems have their limits. Under today's tax code, the only way the feds can raise compliance is to place extraordinary burdens on taxpayers. Most of those financial and social costs also end up being borne by those who already dutifully pay their taxes, in the name of catching the few who evade the law. The tradeoff for higher tax collection is less liberty, as we learned only a decade ago when Congress held much-hyped hearings on abusive IRS tactics and audits.

Simple Is Better

There is a better way. The more complicated a tax system, the more likely taxpayers won't understand, or will try to dodge the rules. Simple tax regimes, such as a single flat rate, encourage compliance and efficiency, not to mention economic growth. This has been the experience of many Eastern European countries after they imposed a flat tax, and the U.S. had similar jumps in reported tax income from "the rich" following the 1986 tax reform that cut rates and closed loopholes.

At least a few "tax-gap" critics in Washington are beginning to understand all this [Senate Finance Chairman Max Baucus and Senator

Charles Grassley, ranking member of the Committee on Finance] have started pairing the "tax gap" problem with the need to eliminate or simplify the Alternative Minimum Tax (AMT)—which is hitting more and more Americans. House Ways and Means Chairman Charlie Rangel has also said that fixing the AMT might require "a look at the whole tax code." Could it be that even Washington is beginning to understand that fixing the tax mess means starting over?

EVALUATING THE AUTHOR'S ARGUMENTS:

In this viewpoint, the author points to the 17,000-page tax-code as the reason that most honest taxpayers make honest mistakes on their taxes. In the previous viewpoint, the author suggests that this same tax code can "veil" (hide) tax-avoidance scams. In your opinion, what are the pros and cons of simplifying the tax code? What might happen if the current tax code was replaced with an entirely new tax code? Give reasons for your answers.

Businesses Cheat

Kevin Smith

In this viewpoint, the author argues that greed is the driving force behind cheating by business executives. The author explains that ethics and honesty often take a back-seat to shareholders' demands for increased growth. Kevin Smith, author of this viewpoint, is the business editor for the *San Gabriel Valley Tribune*, from which this viewpoint was taken.

> "Organizations are more likely to punish unethical behavior that results in personal gain than unethical behavior that results in corporate gain."

AS YOU READ, CONSIDER THE FOLLOWING QUESTIONS:
1. According to this viewpoint, research has shown what correlation between grade point averages and future success?
2. In this viewpoint, what did Gary Kaplan observe about people moving in and out of corporate America?
3. According to this viewpoint, what were the findings by the International Association of Business Communication Research Foundation?

Thursday's [May 26, 2006] conviction of former Enron executives Kenneth Lay and Jeffrey Skilling offered a sobering glimpse at the deepest depths of corporate greed.

Former Enron CEO Jeff Skilling shows remorse after being sentenced by a federal court in 2006 to 24 years and 4 months in federal prison for 19 counts of fraud, conspiracy, insider trading, and lying to auditors.

In a nation where revelations of financial wrongdoing in the business world have become increasingly common, many are left to wonder how—and when—these people lost their moral compass.

Chris Poulson, a professor of management and human resources at Cal Poly Pomona, offered a theory.

Honesty Begins at Home

"Teaching begins at home," Poulson said. "If you'll do anything for a grade . . . you'll do anything for a buck. Students come out of business schools and universities having downloaded most of their papers from the Web. And they've found devious ways to improve their grades by cheating on exams."

How Americans Rate Large U.S. Companies

Having Ethical Business Practices

37% excellent or pretty good

61% only fair or poor

Being Straightforward and Honest in Their Dealings with Consumers and Employees

24% excellent or pretty good

74% only fair or poor

Really Caring About What is Good for America

32% excellent or pretty good

66% only fair or poor

Taken from: Harris Poll, Business Week, September 11, 2000.

Poulson said students and working professionals alike are under increased pressure to produce winning results. And sometimes those results are obtained by questionable means.

"Parental pressure is high and there is also a perception that employers only want people with high grade-point averages," he said. "But research has shown that grade-point averages and future success don't necessarily have any correlation."

In the business world, operations at publicly held companies are heavily shaped by the expectations of shareholders and analysts.

"If we don't meet analyst expectations we're really in trouble," Poulson said.

Ethics Are Disregarded

Gary Kaplan, president of Gary Kaplan & Associates, a Pasadena-based executive search firm, said workplace ethics are being stretched, skewed and in some cases ignored.

"In these contemporary times, there seems to be increased pressure to succeed and accumulate wealth rapidly," Kaplan said. "I think there is an inordinate amount of impatience compared with the last couple of generations."

Kaplan said the traditional concept of working hard, getting periodic merit increases and gradually climbing the corporate ladder has "gone out the window" for many.

That mind-set is reflected in many of the potential job candidates Kaplan's firm sees.

"We deal with a high percentage of individuals who have falsifications on their resumes," he said. "Some don't have the degrees they claim while others claim different majors or grade point averages."

Kaplan said many employees in today's business world are overly eager to get ahead—regardless of how they do it.

Impatience Leads to Cheating

"As an observer of people moving in and out of corporate America, I see there is far less patience to get to that pot of gold," he said. "There is pressure to have the deck stacked in your favor. And if you have that kind of mind-set . . . these are the same kinds of people who play fast and loose with company finances."

Michael Carney, a professor of finance and real estate at Cal Poly Pomona, said most company executives will probably steer clear of any type of questionable behavior.

"I think most of them would want to stay squeaky clean," he said. "These people work very hard to maintain a reputation of integrity, and even suspicion about something like this can cause someone's career to come to a halt. My suspicion is that it's a very small group of people who are doing this."

A newly released survey by the International Association of Business Communicators Research Foundation found 61 percent of companies encourage openness about ethical/unethical conduct in their organizations,

> **FAST FACT**
>
> Citizens for Tax Justice found that 275 of America's largest corporations paid an average tax of 17.3 percent even though the statutory corporate rate is 35 percent. The difference is attributed to special interest laws, shelters, and tax-cheating.

and 46 percent encourage discussion of moral dilemmas and censurable conduct.

Some Businesses Have Two Standards

The survey—which polled 1,827 companies—also noted another particularly disturbing fact: Organizations are more likely to punish unethical behavior that results in personal gain than unethical behavior that results in corporate gain.

Carney thinks Thursday's verdict could do some good in that it might prompt some to abandon money-enriching schemes.

"Those who aren't contemplating fraud of any kind likely won't be affected," he said. "But the ones who are will definitely think twice. Individuals who are inclined toward this type of behavior will be given more to think about."

EVALUATING THE AUTHOR'S ARGUMENTS:

According to this viewpoint, an increasing number of business executives are being exposed as cheaters. Author Kevin Smith raises the question of "how and when these people lost their moral compass." In your opinion—based on what you've learned in this viewpoint and what you know about pressure from parents, bosses, or shareholders—how much influence does outside pressure have on a person's willingness to cheat? Explain the reasons for your answer.

Most Businesses Are Honest

Murray Weidenbaum

In this viewpoint, author Murray Weidenbaum argues that while Enron and other business scandals are causing a low-point in business history, most businesses can be trusted. Weidenbaum says that there are very few lawsuits generated even though millions of business transactions occur daily. Furthermore, Weidenbaum points out that capitalism in America is a self-correcting system that improves itself when it becomes apparent that reforms are needed. Murray Weidenbaum is the Mallinckrodt Distinguished Professor at Washington University and honorary chairman of the Weidenbaum Center on Economy, Government, and Public Policy. This viewpoint, printed in *Executive Speeches*, was originally given in the form of a speech in the Stanley Lyss Lecture Series on ethics.

> *"Most of the time, the [business] system works fairly well."*

AS YOU READ, CONSIDER THE FOLLOWING QUESTIONS:
1. According to the author, what is the most basic example of why he still trusts the business system?
2. According to this viewpoint, what is the acid test of all alternative economic systems?
3. According to the author, back in the eighteenth century, what corrupt business venture did the East India Company engage in?

Murray Weidenbaum, "Business Ethics: Everybody's Favorite Oxymoron," *Executive Speeches*, April-May 2005. Reproduced by permission of the author.

A Google representative demonstrates the search engine's capabilities. Google has become one of the most trustworthy businesses in the modern technological age.

The fact is that the level of business ethics is under serious attack and for very good reason. Almost every day we seem to read about new revelations of corporate malfeasance, accounting fraud, and business conflicts of interest. The wrongdoers are widespread. They have come in every shape, size, and variety. They cover every race, creed, and ethnic group. In the process, many innocent people have lost their reputations, their jobs, and much of their life savings.

That is very discouraging. It should not surprise us that some people have lost faith in the private enterprise system. Personally, I still strongly believe in the benefits of the private enterprise system. But that does not mean that I support the status quo. I strongly believe that we should throw the book at those business officials who let us down and broke or skirted the law. Some laws need to be strengthened and some traditional practices of business need to be overhauled. Yet I think that it is essential that, in examining the changes that are needed, we look at the donut and not just at the hole—or should I say—the bagel.

Business Can Be Trusted

I will start with me most basic example of why I still trust the business system. I can go 10,000 miles to the other end of the globe and count on people who never saw me before and probably never will meet me again to provide me with goods and services in hotels, restaurants, and stores—and they can confidently expect that someone else they never have met will pay them. Less dramatically, I can order from a catalogue and expect the item I requested to arrive without my seeing the person who will send me the item and who will get paid for it by someone else.

Most of the time, the system works fairly well. Of course, like any human activity, the business system does not work perfectly. But, compared to the millions of transactions that occur daily, very few lawsuits are generated in the process. For most of the business transactions I enter into, I can count on the system working.

The American Business System Is Superior

The acid test is that all of the alternative economic systems—feudalism, socialism, communism—have fallen by the wayside. Capitalism does work, despite the presence of greed and other undesirable attributes. Over much of the twentieth century the capitalist nations fed the communist countries. On a more mundane level, when I consider the wide prevalence of bribery and favoritism as a way of life in so many parts of the world, the comparison is quite favorable to the level of ethics in American business, warts and all.

By the way, as someone who has worked in government and the private non-profit sector as well as in business, I have some experience and hence strong views on the subject of the comparative levels of ethics. I have found saints and sinners in each category. I did not find the average levels of ethics in business, government, and university life to be very different. But there is a great range of ethical behavior

> **FAST FACT**
>
> Corporations can legitimately deduct many business expenses to reduce taxable profits, including operating expenses, salaries, bonuses, advertising, and costs associated with medical and retirement plans.

Small Businesses Top the List in 2007 Public Confidence Poll

Type of Business	Public Confidence			
	A Great Deal	Only Some	Hardly Any	Not Sure/ Refused
Small businesses	54%	42%	3%	1%
The military	46%	33%	19%	1%
Major educational institutions such as colleges and universities	37%	50%	12%	1%
Medicine	37%	45%	17%	1%
Organized religion	27%	45%	25%	3%
The U.S. Supreme Court	27%	54%	17%	2%
Public schools	22%	50%	27%	1%
The White House	22%	34%	44%	1%
The courts and the justice system	21%	52%	26%	1%
Television news	20%	54%	25%	1%
Wall Street	17%	51%	24%	7%
Major companies	16%	58%	25%	1%
Organized labor	15%	49%	31%	5%
Law firms	13%	54%	30%	2%
The press	12%	49%	38%	1%
Congress	10%	53%	36%	1%

Taken from: "Confidence in Leaders of Major Institutions: Small Business Tops the List This Year," Harris Poll, March 1, 2007.

in each sector of society. Perhaps the evil doers in business—as well as in government—can do more harm than a professor at a blackboard, but I will not pursue that aspect tonight.

Business Ethics Cycle

Some historical perspective is also useful. Enron may have been a high point—or rather a very low point—in business behavior, but it did not invent business corruption and chicanery. Back in the 18th century, while working at the East India Company, Robert Clive accumulated a personal fortune of 280,000 pounds (that was a multimillionaire's fortune in those days; a pound was really worth a pound). Clive successfully transferred all of his ill-gotten gains from India to England. Worse than that, employees of the East India company sold opium to China and smuggled into Europe the goods they received in turn. In one of the worst examples of Western imperialism, England used its military power to force China to accept and use the opium. Talk about a modern military-industrial complex!

The economic historian Charles Kindleberger also reminds us that, in the nineteenth century, business corruption was so much a fact of life that it became a prominent theme for popular novels. He cites the works of Balzac, Dickens, Thackeray, Trollope, Dumas, Zola—and our own Mark Twain.

The twentieth century produced its full quota of villains. The Boston swindler Charles Ponzi obtained a special type of immortality. He invented the infamous Ponzi scheme. The Teapot Dome scandal in the Harding Administration was a vivid reminder of how low personal behavior in government could fall. Back in the private sector, Bernie Cornfeld created and looted Investors Overseas Services. Ironically, supposed savior Robert Vesco outdid Cornfeld in outright stealing the money of the investors.

American Businesses Reform Themselves

None of this is meant to be an apology for the shortcomings of the status quo. Rather, each of these episodes led to reforms changing prevailing business practices. At least temporarily, those reforms restored public confidence in business. This historical discussion is a prelude to my fundamental point: we must raise the prevailing level of ethics in our private, as well as public, activities.

Moreover, I start off with a positive and not a negative outlook. In good measure, that is because any study of the history of American business demonstrates the continued ability of the system to change and improve itself.

EVALUATING THE AUTHOR'S ARGUMENTS:

Murray Weidenbaum states that episodes of extreme cheating in the past have led to business reforms. In his opinion, this resulted in the restoration of public confidence. In the prior viewpoint, the author stated that shareholders have put immense pressure on businesses to show profits and that pressure sometimes results in cheating. Using what you've learned from both viewpoints—what difficulties might arise when businesses try to please both the shareholders (investors) and the public (customers). Give reasons for your answer.

Chapter 2

Why Do People Cheat?

In January 1999, president Bill Clinton proceeded with his duties to the country while awaiting his impeachment trial by the Senate. It was the first presidential impeachment trial in 130 years.

Athletes Cheat Because of Self-Centeredness

Jon Saraceno

> *"Self-centeredness is reflected in the philosophy of It's All About Me."*

According to this viewpoint, some cheating by athletes has always occurred. The author argues that today, however, cheating is more pervasive. He states that athletes are no longer content to be No. 1, they also want to be the "best compensated" and the "most lauded." The author maintains that this extreme self-centeredness is fueled by the current "money-celebrity" culture in America. Jon Saraceno is a sports columnist and author of this viewpoint which appeared in *USA Today*, the most widely read newspaper in the United States.

AS YOU READ, CONSIDER THE FOLLOWING QUESTIONS:

1. According to this viewpoint, David Callahan, author of the book *The Cheating Culture*, has what thesis about incentives for cheating?
2. According to the author, what other countries besides America have a fascination with pseudo-heroes and cheating?
3. According to this viewpoint, our most feted conquerors are those who win what race?

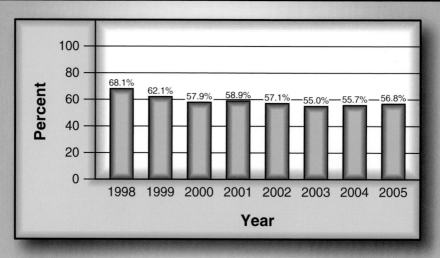

Taken from: 2005 Monitoring the Future Survey, National Institute on Drug Abuse.

Cheating is part of humanity. When it comes to dishonesty in sports, the venerated Greeks were gold medal worthy of guilt thousands of years ago. In baseball, cunning underhandedness is sacrosanct. And when it comes to taxes and speed limits, who shall be the first to cast a stone at the moral minority? So, cheating isn't disappearing anytime soon.

Many experts believe cheating—or "trickeration" in the fractured syntax of [boxing promoter] Don King—is more pervasive. That alone should be troubling enough if you're a sports fan who insists on a level playing field.

I don't know if world-class cyclist Floyd Landis, the son of Mennonites, cheated to win the Tour de France. I'm not sure we'll ever know, even when the next result of his urine sample is released. Landis will forever deny he knowingly took anything that abnormally altered his body's testosterone ratio. The same with world champion sprinter Justin Gatlin, who faces a possible ban after flunking a drug test and a coach claimed a therapist rubbed testosterone cream on his legs without his knowledge. (Only slightly more believable than [baseball player] Barry Bonds' flaxseed oil defense.)

Cheaters Are Self-Centered

What drives much of this competitive overdrive is not only the stated goal to be No. 1, but to be the best compensated and most lauded. That self-centeredness is reflected in the philosophy of It's All About Me.

More people seem driven to commit various forms of integrity suicide and, in the case of those who use performance-enhancing drugs, perhaps unintentional medical chaos. A couple of years ago, noted business author and lecturer David Callahan wrote the book *The Cheating Culture: Why More Americans Are Doing Wrong to Get Ahead.* His thesis is that incentives for betraying honorable behavior are more lucrative—that cheating is now a rational endeavor because of what is at stake, and if everyone's doing it, why not me?

"Nothing is conclusive about Landis right now, but cycling is one of the most drug-saturated sports in the world," he said. "I think that the logic for many cyclists has been, 'Hey, the real rules of the game are that you dope.' It's a pharmacological arms-race. As the financial rewards in sports escalate beyond anything we've ever seen before, we shouldn't be surprised that more people will cut corners to obtain them."

Cheating Is a Worldwide Problem

It isn't only Americans who have a death grip on deceit and deception, despite our fascination with pseudo-heroes who juiced their way to prosperity. Suspected cheaters come in all stripes and occupations. In the Philippines, a widening scandal involves cheating on nursing board exams. In India, scam artists have sold access to test answers for medical students.

In England, one league soccer boss—annoyed by a World Cup riddled with phony injury tactics—has sworn to crack down on fakery.

Competition can be a wonderful thing. In sports, we can think

Athletes who want to be recognized worldwide are more likely to become steroid abusers.

of hundreds of examples of intense nose-to-nose battles that delivered thrills for millions. Watching our favorite players perform acts of supreme athleticism is something to behold and applaud, particularly when it is genuine and minus illegal chemistry.

Competition without moral conscience is something else. Or haven't you noticed those pop-ups on your computer offering instant graduate-course degrees?

A poll of 25,000 U.S. high school students revealed nearly half concurred with this statement: "A person has to lie or cheat sometimes in order to succeed."

Increasingly, students plagiarize. They use test banks and cyber-essays and pop drugs to remain alert. In some ways, none of this is new—the techniques only are more sophisticated. I recall one guy in my high school Spanish class who got busted for "fudging" on a grammar quiz. He scribbled a couple of verb conjugations—on his desk. (I guess l could've been dumber, but I don't know how.)

People Cheat for Prizes and Money

In search of lucrative journalism prizes, some reporters fabricate stories. CEOs finagle accounting methods to fictionalize greater profits, artificially pump up stock prices and trigger bonuses.

Consequently, our most feted conquerors are those who win the race toward massive accumulation of wealth and assets. We are fascinated by conspicuous consumption, intrigued by the power of those phony captains of industry who are really lowly first mates in their own self-absorption and ultimate destruction.

"The money-celebrity culture has changed people's values and elevated ends over means," Callahan said. "You have a natural human impulse to (gain an unfair advantage) filtered through changing incentives and societal values, which I suggest creates more cheating. It's a self-fulfilling dynamic. People think they need to cheat just to compete on an even field."

I asked him if he were offered a [psychoactive] drug that would enable him to write a Pulitzer Prize-winning book, would he ingest it? "Good question," he said.

"Yeah, I probably would."

He is honest, which is a lot more than some athletes. Then again, that only makes them more like us.

> **EVALUATING THE AUTHOR'S ARGUMENTS:**
>
> In this viewpoint, the author states that self-centeredness is behind the pervasive cheating by athletes. Based on the arguments in this viewpoint, if a society heaps inordinate amounts of fame and fortune on a few top athletes—is society contributing to the "win at all costs" (cheating) behavior? Also, in your opinion, do Americans really want fake heroes? Explain your answers.

Athletes Cheat to Level the Playing Field

Jeff Barker

"I began using substances not to give me an advantage, but because I had become convinced I needed to use them to level the playing field."

In this viewpoint, the author cites the case of Kelli White, who in 2003 held two world titles in sprinting. White later admitted to using steroids and told the House Government Reform Committee that she didn't use the substances to give herself an advantage (the definition of cheating), but to level the playing field. In contrast, the author cites the case of John Godina, a two-time Olympic medalist, who never used steroids, but was beaten more than once by athletes who later tested positive for performance-enhancing drugs. Jeff Barker is a reporter for the *Baltimore Sun,* from which this viewpoint was taken.

AS YOU READ, CONSIDER THE FOLLOWING QUESTIONS:
1. According to John Godina, quoted in this viewpoint, what factors can influence an athlete into using or forgoing illegal substances?

2. According to a recent book cited in this viewpoint, how did Barry Bonds feel about performance-enhancing drugs?
3. According to the author, what confusing messages does society send to athletes?

John Godina, 34, a two-time Olympic medalist in shot put . . . recalled winning the silver medal at the tainted 1997 world championships in Athens, Greece.

Amid swirling rumors, Godina got a call a few days after the competition telling him that the man ahead of him, Aleksandr Bagach of the Ukraine, was being disqualified for taking stimulants. Godina was declared the gold medal winner, but he said it wasn't the same as if he had won it in the stadium:

"It would have been nice to take that victory lap, to wave to the fans and get the medal at the podium," Godina said. The third-place finisher, fellow American C.J. Hunter, later retired as a shot putter after positive steroid tests.

Honest Athletes Are Defeated by Cheaters

Godina says he has come to accept that he will occasionally be defeated by rivals who later test positive, either immediately or sometime in the future. "It's happened over and over," he said.

Godina, who says he has never been tempted by steroids, says there are several factors that can influence an athlete into using or forgoing illegal substances.

"A lot of it depends on who you surround yourself with. If people constantly tell you you're only losing because you're not using, it can eat away at you," Godina says.

FAST FACT

Ancient Greek Olympians ingested ram testicles to enhance their performance.

He says confidence is also a determinant: "If you have success early, you think you can succeed without some help."

Says Washington Nationals catcher Brian Schneider: "It comes down to how good you feel about yourself."

[David] Callahan [author of the book *The Cheating Culture*] says

Side Effects of Performance-enhancing Drugs

According to the National Coalition for the Advancement of Drug-free Athletes: *"Up to 500,000 student-athletes are currently using some type of performance-enhancing drug."*

Possible Side-effects for Males	Possible Side-effects for Females
• Shrinking of testicles	• Growth of facial hair
• Impotence	• Male pattern baldness
• Bad temper (roid rage)	• Change or cessation of menstrual cycle
• Development of breasts	• Breast reduction
• Increased risk of prostate cancer	• Deepened voice

Taken from: The National Coalition for the Advancement of Drug-free Athletes.

society is ruled by undermanned, often ineffective regulatory watchdogs that allow cheating to flourish. And, he says, cheating seems to perpetuate itself.

Cheaters Use Performance-Enhancing Drugs

Consider the case of Kelli White, the former sprinter who won the 100- and 200-meter world titles in 2003. The next year, she admitted taking steroids and received a two-year competition ban from the U.S. Anti-Doping Agency. She had passed 17 drug tests before being confronted with a cache of evidence that included drug-use schedules and incriminating e-mails.

In her ultra-competitive world, White had believed she needed to cheat to keep up.

"I believe it is important that you understand the reasons I made the choice to, in essence, cheat," she told the House Government Reform Committee last year. "I began using these substances not to give me an advantage, but because I had become convinced I needed to use them to level the playing field with my competitors."

White's reasoning may have paralleled that of San Francisco Giants

Kelli White, former world champion sprinter, discusses how doping affected her athletic career, citing that she used performance-enhancing drugs only to help level the playing field against other athletes.

slugger Barry Bonds. According to a recent book, Bonds, who has denied using performance-enhancing drugs, was consumed by jealousy when he first decided to use performance-enhancing drugs. The book, by two San Francisco Chronicle reporters, says Bonds was irate in 1998 over the attention given the power-hitting feats of Mark McGwire and [Sammy] Sosa.

McGwire has declined to answer questions about whether he used steroids during his career. Sosa told a congressional panel last year: "I have never taken performance-enhancing drugs."

Judging Cheaters Is Complicated

Callahan says the "other people were doing it" defense doesn't clear an offender of wrongdoing, although it does make judging them more complicated. "What if [a banned practice] becomes so common that even honest people need to do it to keep up? Then the ethics of it become very murky," the author says. "But not everybody does cheat."

White had once contemplated a comeback when her suspension ended. But her agent, Jerrold Colton, said this week that she has abandoned such thoughts.

"She's pretty much retired," Colton said. "She was just accepted into an MBA program and she's looking to move ahead with her life."

Experts say society sends confusing messages to athletes such as White. American culture places a disproportionate emphasis on coming out ahead—and on fame—often at the expense of ethics, says Syracuse University popular culture expert Robert Thompson.

In fact, Thompson says, society holds a special place for charismatic cheaters.

People Admire Cheaters

"There is a sense, I think, that we have increasingly gotten more and more tolerance for the outlaw," Thompson says. "It wasn't that long ago that we went from heroes like John Wayne—honest as the day is long—to Butch Cassidy and the Sundance Kid, who were the outlaws."

Says Callahan: "We worship the winners as never before with this 24-7 celebrity culture. None of the heroes these days are people trying to make the world a better place. Our heroes are people like Donald Trump and Paris Hilton."

Given society's ambiguity, Thompson said it's understandable that a figure like Bonds, second on the all-time home run list, is booed by some and applauded by others. He said some fans may praise Bonds for rising to the top of his profession, some may consider him a cheat, and some are likely torn.

"There are a lot of people conflicted about Barry Bonds," Thompson said.

EVALUATING THE AUTHOR'S ARGUMENTS:

In this viewpoint, the author quotes a question raised by David Callahan: "What if [a banned practice] becomes so common that even honest people need to do it to keep up?" Using what you learned in this viewpoint and the previous viewpoint, decide if you agree or disagree with the idea that honest people sometimes need to cheat. Then, give three reasons to support your decision.

Students Cheat Because Teachers Are Unfair

Bill Puka

> *"If I had to cite a single regret of my own student history, it would be failing to cheat when I was being victimized by unfair testing and grading."*

In this viewpoint, author Bill Puka combines his experience as both a student and a college professor to share some rare insights on student cheating. He contends that some teachers purposely oppress students by being hard-graders and giving exams that are designed to frustrate or fail students. In his opinion, this and other abusive teaching techniques encourages cheating. Furthermore, Puka argues, amidst such oppressive practices, students sometimes have an obligation to cheat, if for no other reason than to preserve their own self-respect. Bill Puka obtained his PhD at Harvard University in philosophy and psychology and currently teaches ethics at Rensselaer Polytechnic Institute.

AS YOU READ, CONSIDER THE FOLLOWING QUESTIONS:

1. In the author's opinion, willingness to sully our purity to fight wrongs indicates what about our commitment?
2. According to the author, how can teachers make it nearly impossible for students to cheat or to plagiarize?

Bill Puka, "Student Cheating," *Liberal Education*, summer-fall 2005, pp. 32-35. Reproduced by permission.

If I had to cite a single regret of my own student history, it would be failing to cheat when I was being victimized by unfair testing and grading, not to mention abusive teaching overall. In submitting to this treatment, I showed undue conventionalism and acquiescence in petty tyranny, both of which are toxic to ethical integrity. True, I often protested such unfair treatment. But this invariably worked to my detriment and that of my peers. (No de facto, due-process option is available for winning such protests.) Worse, my protest was viewed as courageous, as properly standing up for principle. The courage I really needed to learn was that of dirtying one's hands a bit, adjusting my general principles to the specific context of unjust treatment. I needed the distinctive moral courage to besmirch my personal virtue in hopes of subverting injustice and its harms.

One comes to learn that those willing to sully their purity to fight wrongs show a level of moral commitment that rises well above nobility. After all, nobility normally requires conspiring, if not purposely, in the oppressive practices of others. In the present case, it means failing to expose poor teaching and its misrepresentation as students' failure to learn. Adult morality demands "principled" flexibility, not personal consistency masquerading as character. At the college level especially, ethics education can cleave toward the adult, though it presently does not, transcending childhood devices like codes of conduct or "do-and-don't" rules.

Fast Fact

In 2004 Mississippi threw out a portion of test scores at nine schools after discovering two dozen cases of alleged cheating.

Some Teachers Victimize Students

Some faculty actually boast about their bad teaching behavior, and they are admired for it by their colleagues. They proudly depict themselves as "hard-nosed graders" who give "killer exams," which many fail and almost all do poorly on. This is a self-indicting outrage. A competent teacher makes course material sing and partners with students in skill development. If students do not do top-notch work, then either they are not functioning primarily as students in the course or the teaching approach taken needs radical change.

With a little thought and effort, most faculty can make it well-nigh impossible for students to cheat or plagiarize. One way is by not giving the same exams repeatedly. Another is by not using multiple-choice or other mechanical examination formats. A third is by asking students to do several drafts of a paper, illustrating the developing process of their work on each task, and integrating progressive drafts incrementally. (One searches the Web in vain for papers satisfying these requirements.) Add an oral, face-to-face component to the drafting process and the learning involved simply can't be faked or simulated.

Better Teaching Takes More Time

Such "progressive" measures can take more faculty effort and time than do standard tests. But isn't that what "hard-headed teachers and graders" expect of their students? Why not of themselves also? Measurement batteries that get at the full variety of student learning and effort have long been available. Why then do faculty cling to the long outmoded and discredited in their course practices? (Unfortunately, this rhetorical question has an all-too-pragmatic answer: college faculty must decrease teaching and grading time relative to research and grant-making activities. This response is ethically self-indicting as well—for faculty and administrators.)

Isn't such negligent or disingenuous teaching more ethically problematic than student cheating? . . .

Unfair Teachers Disrespect Students

Ethicists who are incensed by student cheating show no similar concern for the rampant disrespect shown students, nor for the extreme anxiety caused them when inflexible deadlines are mandated for class assignments or when faculty assign exams and papers that are all due at the same time. A complete lack of coordination is clear here among faculty in different courses and departments, with a lack of concern even to try. Students suffer prolonged and painful loneliness at college, especially at first, and periods of isolating alienation from peers. They anguish alone with crises of identity and the loss of spiritual orientation, personal meaning, and self-worth. Conflicts with parents and the breakup of love relationships often rob them of interest and motivation, sapping the power to concentrate on studies. The real harm, the real suffering involved here often gets recorded as poor classroom achievement. Were institutions actually fostering the kind of community and the sense of belonging they advertise, along with the social skills mentioned in descriptions of campus "leadership" programs, these evils could be mitigated. Yet instead of addressing

Some students claim that hard-grading teachers and social pressures lead to cheating in the classroom.

such institutional failings openly and responsibly, the blame is shifted to the emotional problems of particular students. And these problems are treated confidentially through individual counseling outside the curriculum.

Violations Are Handled Unfairly

A last puzzler: at most universities, students are banished from their learning community for cheating and plagiarism. The unwitting ethical lesson taught here is that enlightened and reflective communities handle internal messes by sweeping them outside. They handle rule violations and significant faults in their members by changing the locks on the doors. If the student offense is small, expulsion is replaced by "hard labor," usually in the form of assigned research on academic honesty. Here the ideals of inquiry are portrayed as a form of punishment, and student suspicions about the real nature of "school work" are affirmed.

Notwithstanding the above tally, some colleges and universities show that higher education can get serious about ethics education. All can do so, potentially, by putting their own houses in order as an example to their students.

EVALUATING THE AUTHOR'S ARGUMENTS:

In this viewpoint, the author states that poor and oppressive teaching techniques can be misrepresented as students' failure to learn. In other words, a teacher's "killer exams" and incompetent teaching can cheat students out of grades that they deserve. In your opinion, does this therefore give students the right to cheat their teacher? Give reasons to support your answer.

Student Cheating Is the Result of Cultural Norms

Emily Flynn Vencat, Jason Overdorf, and Jonathan Adams

"We've passed the tipping point, where cheating is so common that it's an accepted social norm."

In this viewpoint, the authors state that student cheating is not only accepted, it is admired. They point to the prevalence of using electronic devices to cheat, and argue that students feel pressure to cheat in order to compete for top colleges. Emily Flynn Vencat, a Special Correspondent for Newsweek International, and writers Jason Overdorf of New Delhi and Jonathan Adams of Taipei teamed up to author this viewpoint.

AS YOU READ, CONSIDER THE FOLLOWING QUESTIONS:

1. According to this viewpoint, how have technological advances made cheating easier than ever?
2. According to this viewpoint, how does the upsurge in school dishonesty reflect the attitude of the culture at large?
3. In this viewpoint, how are European exams being armed against plagiarism?

C hris doesn't consider himself a cheater. Yet for the past four years, the 21-year-old senior at one of California's most prestigious universities (which he doesn't want identified) has used an arsenal of tricks to pass his classes. He's plagiarized, taken illegal prescription drugs to improve his focus, obtained exam questions in advance and text-messaged his friends via cell phone to find quick answers to tough questions. Still, he doesn't see any of that as out of the ordinary. "Sure, I've used test banks, study drugs, text buddies, cyberessays and picture messaging," he says. "But so does everyone."

That may be an exaggeration—but not as big of one as you might think. From Beijing to Bristol, the rates of academic cheating have skyrocketed during the past decade. In a huge study of 50,000 college and 18,000 high-school students in the United States by Duke University's Center for Academic Integrity, more than 70 percent admitted to having cheated. That's up from about 56 percent in 1993 and just

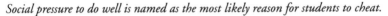

Social pressure to do well is named as the most likely reason for students to cheat.

26 percent in 1963. Internet plagiarism has quadrupled in the past six years, according to the same study. In Britain, a recent government-sponsored report found such rampant cheating in the state-run GCSE and A-level exams that Secretary of Education Ruth Kelly called for a total revamp of the coursework system before 2008. Hundreds of Asian universities' Web-based bulletin boards are dumping grounds for the memorized answers to Test of English as a Foreign Language questions—the basis of most U.S. colleges' admittance of foreign students.

Student Cheating Is a Worldwide Problem

Nearly all of India's ultracompetitive entrance exams have been stolen and sold to students at least once during the past five years. In 2004 students paid up to $15,000 apiece for access to answers to India's Pre-Medical Test—and the perpetrators pocketed $1 million. In China, where the number of university students has almost tripled since 1998 to 16 million, police last year cracked one of the biggest *qiangshou* (hired gun) gangs—Web-based agencies where students can hire expert look-alikes to take any of a host of national exams for them. The gang had already taken in $212,000 from nearly 1,000 students in 19 provinces across the country. Also in 2005, South Korea faced the biggest exam-cheating scandal in its history when officials realized that the previous fall's national college-entrance exam, the CSAT, had been infiltrated by more than 20 cheating rings across the country; they had text-messaged exam answers to paying students taking the test. "We've passed the tipping point, where cheating is so common that it's an accepted social norm," says David Callahan, author of *The Cheating Culture*.

What's turning students into crooks? First and foremost, technological advances have made cheating easier than ever. From purchasing "original" essays from Web sites like Gradesaver.com to "outsourcing" computer-programming homework to experts in India via sites like Rentacoder.com, students can now buy A's for the price of a school lunch. At the same time, mobile phones and MP3 players have given test takers new tools: picture messaging lets them contact friends outside the classroom with photographed copies of whole exams. SparkMobile, a new service from SparkNotes (Barnes & Noble's take on Cliffs Notes), will text students themes to use for surprise in-class essays or beam them iPod-friendly audio summaries of classic novels.

Intense Competition Causes Cheating

Competition, though, is the real culprit. As the work force becomes ever more crowded and the number of college grads skyrockets, top educational credentials are increasingly seen as the only sure vehicle to success. Thirty-five years ago, just 11 percent of Americans had a college degree; now nearly a third do. In the European Union, the number of university graduates has shot up by 30 percent in the past five years alone. In hypercompetitive Asia, where most academic achievement is measured by standardized tests, that can lead to excruciating pressure. "Your exams are so closely connected to your admission to college that a 0.1 percent difference can determine whether you get admitted or not," says Sudha Ravi, vice principal at a prestigious New Delhi secondary school.

Sociologists argue that the upsurge in school dishonesty also reflects attitudes in the culture at large, where cheating has become acceptable and even admired. International tycoons make enviable fortunes through market manipulation and fraud: think Enron, WorldCom and Martha Stewart. Scientists like South Korea's once revered stem-cell research pioneer, Hwang Woo Suk, fake lab results. In a recent poll of 25,000 high-schoolers by the California-based Josephson Institute of Ethics, nearly half agreed with the statement "A person has to lie or cheat sometimes in order to succeed." In Australia, a new study from Griffith University of students at four major campuses revealed that 40 percent believe faking research results is a "minor" offense. "Students feel like it's just no longer a big deal to cheat," says Don McCabe, the founder of Duke University's Center for Academic Integrity.

Cheating Results in Test Reform

The problem is so pervasive that it's reshaping the face of academic admissions. In the future, exams from the SAT to the MCAT to the A-levels will be administered in secure rooms equipped with metal detectors, radio-frequency locators to check if students are receiving text-messaged answers on their mobile phones and, in China and South Korea at least, the threat of up to seven-year prison sentences for cheats. This year the world's most respected graduate entrance test, the GRE, which is taken by half a million students annually, is undergoing the biggest face-lift in its 55-year history. Starting this October, exam questions will be changed from test to test. Start times will be staggered across the globe so students in Los Angeles

can't post memorized or photographed test sheets on the Web for students in Hong Kong. "We've basically revolutionized the way we're administering our high-stakes tests," says Ray Nicosia, director of security for the world's largest test administrator, the Princeton, New

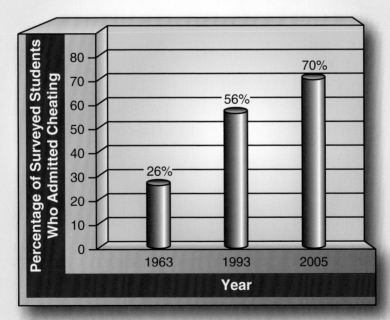

Most Students Cheat

According to a study of 50,000 college and 18,000 high school students in the Duke University's Center for Academic Integrity, more than 70 percent admitted to having cheated.

Percentage of Surveyed Students Who Admitted Cheating

- 1963: 26%
- 1993: 56%
- 2005: 70%

Year

Taken from: Center for Academic Integrity, Duke University.

Jersey-based Educational Testing Service, which runs 25,000 test centers in 192 countries. "We're changing to combat this problem."

America's med-school entrance exam, the MCAT, is stepping up security measures using biometrics. As of next year, would-be doctors will have to give electronic fingerprints and submit to digital photographs, making it easier for exam boards to catch cheaters who pay others to take the tests for them. The SAT last year added a writing section which, says Nicosia, provides a "substantive handwriting exemplar" to authenticate test takers. South Korea's Ministry of Education has introduced metal detectors for bathroom visits. In India, testing bodies have limited the number of administrators with early access to the exams.

European exams like Britain's GCSE and A-levels and France's baccalaureate are arming themselves with plagiarism-spotting software, like TurnItIn.com and MyDropBox.com, which compare student papers with everything available on the Internet and highlight copied sections in bright red. Some top institutions in the United States and Europe have even "legalized cheating." They now allow students to surf the Web on PDAs and laptops during "open Internet" exams. Proponents argue that this helps students learn research skills more applicable to real-life work situations, where information is freely available.

Interviews May Replace Tests

At the same time, a growing number of top universities are reducing their emphasis on standardized tests. Many are even beginning to throw them out altogether in favor of interviews and recommendations—markers of aptitude that can't be faked. The rising incidence of scoring errors has only heightened their concerns; just two weeks ago the U.S. College Board revealed that some 4,000 scores from last October's SAT had been miscalculated—some by as much as 400 points. "I do see a rise in alternative ways to augment the scores," says Gary Natriello, an education professor at Columbia University's Teachers College. "People are looking for those other signs that a student has a lot of potential."

Will standardized tests ever become obsolete? According to the Massachusetts-based National Center for Fair & Open Testing, some 730 American colleges no longer require undergrad applicants to take either the SAT or the ACT. In Britain, Oxford and Cambridge used to interview top candidates once; now final decisions are made after two interviews. Marlyn McGrath Lewis, the director of admissions for Harvard College, says more and more universities are adopting a "holistic approach to admissions"—and that's essential. "The quality of [the class] depends on it." Not to mention the quality of the education.

EVALUATING THE AUTHORS' ARGUMENTS:

In this viewpoint, the authors blame skyrocketing student cheating "first and foremost" on technological advances. In contrast, in the previous viewpoint, author Bill Puka blamed poor teaching. He said, "With a little thought and effort, most faculty (teachers) can make it well-nigh impossible for students to cheat or to plagiarize." Based on the arguments presented in these two viewpoints and what you know about cheating, what is the primary cause of increased student cheating: teachers or technology? Explain your answer.

Relationship Cheating Is Caused By Unclear Boundaries

Peggy Ann Torney

"Emotional affairs are deceptive activities that can undermine marriages and other serious relationships."

According to this viewpoint, many couples are unaware that outside friendships can escalate into emotional affairs. Emotional affairs, which involve no physical contact, can be just as destructive to a committed relationship as physical affairs. The author argues that emotional affairs are still cheating. According to the author, these affairs differ from healthy friendships outside the marriage because they exclude the significant other and involve deceit. Peggy Ann Torney wrote this viewpoint for the *Toronto Star*, Canada's largest daily newspaper.

AS YOU READ, CONSIDER THE FOLLOWING QUESTIONS:
1. According to the author, many people in committed relationships are unaware of what?

Peggy Ann Torney, "Couples Face A Growing Threat: Emotional Infidelity," *Columbia News Service*, December 27, 2005. Reproduced by permission of Columbia News Service.

2. According to this viewpoint, experts say men and women enter into the danger zone at what point?
3. According to the author, appeal of online affairs can serve as a signal of what problem?

For years, S., a married woman, was happy coming home from work with a bag of groceries and plans for the evening meal. Lately, though, she is more likely to race through the front door empty-handed, tell her husband by phone that she will be ordering in and sit eagerly before the computer.

She is excited to learn that a particular male friend is online. Like a scene from the romantic comedy *Must Love Dogs*, S. tells her cyber pal about her day, shares her hopes, fears and fantasies and, sometimes, talks about her husband.

Emotional cheating is one of many grey areas in the infidelity between a man and a woman.

When she hears her husband's key in the lock, S. signs off the computer and comes to the door. He asks about her day. "Fine," she says, "but I don't really feel like talking about it."

Although S. is not involved sexually with her online friend, her husband does have reason to worry. S. is having an emotional affair.

Emotional Affairs Are Destructive

Many people in committed relationships aren't aware that emotional affairs can be as intense and destructive as physical ones. Men usually recognize an affair only if it becomes sexual, says John Gray, author of *Men Are From Mars, Women Are From Venus*. Since women connect love with emotional support, they generally feel more threatened by emotional affairs.

Emotional affairs are deceptive activities that can undermine marriages and other serious relationships. Experts agree it is the deceit and betrayal that cause the most damage.

Experts say men and women enter the danger zone when they begin to exclude their significant other, keep aspects of their friendship secret and engage in deeply intimate or sensual conversations with their cyber friend.

"If your partner knows everything about your friendship, it's probably okay. If they don't, it's probably not," says Peggy Vaughan of DearPeggy.com, a website that provides information and support for couples trying to sort their way through the aftermath of an affair.

Emotional Affairs Rob the Significant Other

Says M. Gary Neuman, author of *Emotional Infidelity: How to Affair-Proof Your Marriage and 10 Other Secrets to a Great Relationship*: "You may not cheat physically, but the fact that you are using energy, you are robbing your primary relationship of energy it needs."

Of course, these cyber affairs do not have to be the death of a relationship.

Five Tips That He's About to Cheat (or already has):

1. He's distant.

2. He picks fights.

3. His friends are acting weird.

4. He wants to know your every move.

5. He puts you down.

Taken from: Kierna Mayo, "Cheat Sheet," Cosmo Girl, October 2005.

"The appeal of online affairs can serve as a signal that we need to rethink all aspects of our lives and determine what we can do to feel more 'alive,'" Vaughan says.

Gray says couples should tap the origins of the affair and infuse the marriage with some of that excitement.

Emotional Affairs Are a Wake-up Call

If acknowledged and dealt with, emotional affairs can shake couples out of their lethargy and force them to face what's missing in their relationships, the experts says.

"Put all you've got into your relationship," Neuman says, "and you'll have it all—everything you could realistically hope for and even more than you could ever imagine."

EVALUATING THE AUTHOR'S ARGUMENTS:

This viewpoint begins by contrasting a woman's relationship with her husband before and after she enters into an illicit emotional affair. Based on the information in this viewpoint, in your opinion, can an emotional affair be as devastating to a committed relationship as a physical affair? Please give reasons for your answers.

Relationship Cheating Is Facilitated by New Technology

Mark de la Vina

"Technology has helped the cause, prompting the curious to make the jump from fantasy to philandering."

In the following viewpoint, the author explains why new technology has contributed to increased relationship cheating. Computers, cell phones, and online dating services make it easier to initiate and maintain illicit affairs. Furthermore, he argues that innocent users of technology are bombarded with slick spam messages that can entice curious, but otherwise faithful, people into exploring cheating websites. Mark de la Vina is the arts, entertainment and style reporter for the *San Jose Mercury News,* from which this viewpoint was taken.

AS YOU READ, CONSIDER THE FOLLOWING QUESTIONS:
1. According to this viewpoint, while no reliable figures exist on the increase of cheaters who use technology, what is undeniable?
2. According to the author, an online dating service based in Toronto specifically targets what type of user?

3. According to this viewpoint, some people, given the proper social boundaries, would be less likely to do what?

Cheating is on the rise because technology eases the search to find a willing partner, according to therapists, researchers and relationship experts. The unfaithful no longer have to scour bars or cultivate workplace relationships. Cheating has increased along with the growing use of text messaging and cell phones, chat rooms and online dating sites, some exclusively targeting the polygamous.

"The Internet has greatly removed the barriers," says Ruth Houston, founder of Infidelityadvice.com and author of *Is He Cheating on You? 829 Telltale Signs*. "If you are a married person who wants to cheat, you can now go online and maintain an affair even while your spouse is in the room. Everything has changed."

Jill, 45, an elementary school teacher from Mountain View who asked that her last name not be used, learned of her partner's infidelity when she came across his open e-mail account, which he had failed

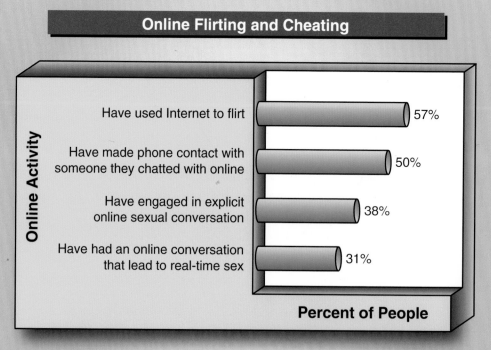

Online Flirting and Cheating

Online Activity

- Have used Internet to flirt — 57%
- Have made phone contact with someone they chatted with online — 50%
- Have engaged in explicit online sexual conversation — 38%
- Have had an online conversation that lead to real-time sex — 31%

Percent of People

to log off on their home computer. She was shocked to read that he had done "everything from soliciting hookers to making dates with others" via the Internet, she says. "I saw that he does this all day at work. I even posed as someone he had been conversing with, and he e-mailed me 30 times in one day!"

When Jill revealed her identity, he downplayed his online trawling, which "ruined our romance," she says.

The Rise in Cheating Is Undeniable

No reliable figures exist on the increase in cheaters who use technology, but computer forensics expert John Lucich says the rise is undeniable. The president of Network Security Group, a firm in Union, N.J., hired for computer-related legal issues, says that 95 percent of the cases his company handles involve men and women who set up secret e-mail accounts for the purpose of cheating.

Online dating sites play a key role in connecting people searching for extracurricular activities. While mainstream services such as Match.com and Yahoo Personals ban married people from posting profiles, the dating sites can't stop users from lying. Other companies are happy to pick up the slack.

Private Affairs (www. philanderers.com), an online dating site based in Toronto, targets users looking for what it calls EMRs, or extramarital relationships. Another service, Ashley Madison Agency (www.ashleymadison.com), boasts 1.03 million members in the United States, Canada and the United Kingdom. With its tag line "when monogamy becomes monotony," the company, also founded in Toronto, has seen its membership double annually, says operations director and founder Darren Morgenstern.

"We're finding that it's just not going away," he says. "People are looking at the plausibility of using the Internet to have an affair, and it just works for them."

Once the connection is made, technology also helps the affair to thrive. Cell phones and PDAs give cheaters the chance to communicate privately and coordinate with their side dish. . . .

It has been suggested that as the Information Age progresses, more people are able to cheat on their significant others more easily.

Technology Expedites Cheating

Technology has helped the cause, prompting the curious to make the jump from fantasy to philandering, says Brian Person, a marriage and family therapist in Los Altos.

"Some people, given the proper social boundaries, would be less likely to cheat than they are now," he says.

Network Security Group's Lucich is convinced that the rise in advertising and e-mail spam that hype cheating sites entice people to cross those boundaries, he says.

"I truly believe that there are people out there who have not thought about infidelity and then get spam messages or hear about online cheating and dating sites on the radio," says Lucich, whose book *Cyber Lies* details how to easily check a partner's cell phone or computer to discover if he or she is cheating. "In a weak moment, they say, 'Let's just take a peek.' Then they start going further and further, and the next thing you know, they're cheating."

EVALUATING THE AUTHOR'S ARGUMENTS:

In this viewpoint, the author states that new technology makes it easier for cheaters to cross clearly defined boundaries by logging on to websites specifically designed to help married people cheat. In contrast, the previous viewpoint highlighted the pitfall of unclear boundaries, where a seemingly innocent friendship can escalate into an emotional affair. In your opinion, which boundary issue contributes most to the rise in relationship cheating: The ease of jumping a clearly defined boundary with new technology or the risk of crossing an unclear boundary when an innocent friendship escalates into an emotional affair? Explain your answer.

Corporate Cheating Stems from Greed

Katherine Mangan

"Greed has fueled a spate of notable corporate scandals— Enron, WorldCom, Arthur Andersen, and Tyco— in recent years."

According to this viewpoint, in the last ten years there has been an increase in corporate scandals due to cheating caused by greed. Some scholars, notes Mangan, believe that business schools are to blame as they teach future business executives that shareholder profits take first priority. Other scholars argue that Americans live in a commercial society where people believe that "money is a measure of one's worth." According to this viewpoint, because of this cultural norm, business schools can't be blamed for executives that take profit making and greed to the extreme. Katherine Mangan is a former editor for the Associated Press and a national correspondent for the *Chronicle of Higher Education,* from which this viewpoint was taken.

AS YOU READ, CONSIDER THE FOLLOWING QUESTIONS:
1. According to this viewpoint, how important is business educations' emphasis on the virtues of maximizing shareholder value?

2. According to the author, while advocates of shareholder primacy say that a focus on the bottom line leads to an efficient company, what do Mr. Khurana and Mr. Gintis have to say?
3. If you don't punish people for breaching ethical standards, according to Richard A. Posner, quoted in this viewpoint, what will happen?

In the movie *Wall Street*, a ruthless and corrupt corporate raider named Gordon Gekko delivers an impassioned speech to a paper company's stockholders that outlines the freewheeling philosophy that has made him rich.

"The point is, ladies and gentlemen, that greed, for lack of a better word, is good," he says. "Greed is right. Greed works—and greed—you mark my words—will not only save Teldar Paper but that other malfunctioning corporation called the U.S.A."

Greed has also fueled a spate of notable corporate scandals—Enron, WorldCom, Arthur Andersen, and Tyco—in recent years.

That trend has some observers arguing that today's business schools, by elevating shareholder profit above social benefits and other concerns, may have unintentionally become breeding grounds for a generation of Gordon Gekkos.

Prominent Cheaters Came from Prominent Schools

After all, prominent Enron executives caught up in that scandal, including the former chief executive, Jeffrey K. Skilling (convicted of fraud and conspiracy) [in May 2006], and the former chief financial officer, Andrew S. Fastow (who pleaded guilty to wire and securities fraud in January 2004), had M.B.A.'s from prominent business schools—Harvard and Northwestern Universities, respectively.

> **FAST FACT**
>
> Half the students in the Aspen Institute MBA Student Attitudes survey anticipate that they will have to make business decisions that conflict with their values. However, according to these same students, less than one out of four are being prepared to manage value conflicts.

Corporate corruption has led many companies into financial and legal ruin.

Business-school leaders, however, say it is not fair to blame institutions for the shady dealings of some of their graduates, though they have introduced a flurry of ethics courses for their students in recent years.

Just as important, they add, is that business education's emphasis on the virtues of maximizing shareholder value is a central pillar of contemporary economic theory, and it remains a useful tool for understanding and resolving conflicts of interest among stockholders, managers, and other players in a company.

It Is Not the Fault of the Schools

Michael C. Jensen, an emeritus professor at Harvard Business School, says that teaching the primacy of the shareholder in corporate thinking doesn't make students corrupt.

"There is no doubt that there have been many more incidents of inappropriate behavior in the business world in the last decade," he says, "but those who attribute that to a problem with the M.B.A. degree or what's being taught in business schools will have a tough time explaining it."

One of Mr. Jensen's former students—Rakesh Khurana, an associate professor of organizational behavior at Harvard Business School—is taking a stab at explaining the link at a symposium on values and free enterprise to be held this week at Harvard. . . .

In a paper to be delivered at the symposium, Mr. Khurana and Herbert Gintis, a game theorist and professor emeritus of economics at the University of Massachusetts at Amherst, observe that "the founders of business schools never envisioned the notion that the sole purpose of the corporation was to serve only one master—the shareholder."

Shareholder Profits Are Overemphasized

While advocates of shareholder primacy say that a focus on the bottom line leads to an efficient and profitable company, Mr. Khurana and Mr. Gintis counter that the theory "creates a corporate atmosphere that legitimizes a culture of greed in which managers are encouraged to care about nothing but personal gain, and in which such human character virtues as honesty and decency are deployed only contingently in the interests of personal material reward."

John J. Fernandes, president and chief executive of AACSB International: the Association to Advance Collegiate Schools of Business, agrees that most business schools have overemphasized the importance of shareholder profits over the past few decades.

But he says ethics and corporate responsibility have made significant inroads into the curricula over the past five years.

"An important theory of business is maximizing profits—companies have that responsibility to shareholders," he says. "But not at any cost. A company's reputation is hard-earned and easily lost.". . .

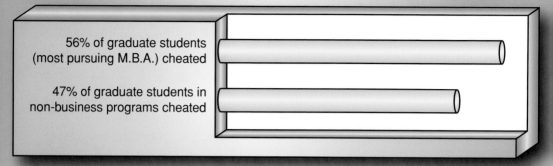

Graduate Business Students Have Higher Prevalence of Cheating

56% of graduate students (most pursuing M.B.A.) cheated

47% of graduate students in non-business programs cheated

Taken from: Katherine Mangan, "Survey Finds Widespread Cheating in M.B.A. Programs," The Chronicle of Higher Education, September 19, 2006.

Cheating Is a Cultural Norm

Some scholars, including Richard A. Posner, a federal judge and senior lecturer in law at the University of Chicago, contend that it is a waste of time to preach to business students about ethics. He believes that students should, however, be taught the boundaries over which ethical lapses cross the line into breaking the law.

"If you don't punish people for breaching ethical standards, those standards aren't going to have much effect," he says. "This is a commercial society. Having money is the surest path to prestige in the United States, and the people who go into business accept this social standard that money is the measure of your worth. You can't expect them to be the first to sacrifice their commercial opportunities in order to make a moral gesture."

Mr. Posner sees nothing wrong with encouraging business students to take ethical stands if it translates to good public relations, and, consequently, a healthier bottom line.

"If you're in a competitive environment, you the manager can't afford to be altruistic in the sense of sacrificing efficiency to achieve social goals," he says. "If you do that, your company will be less profitable, the shareholders will squawk, and you'll lose managers to more profitable companies."

Mr. Gintis and Mr. Khurana argue that business students should have the same sense of social responsibility that members of other professions have. "If you're a doctor, you don't decide how to treat a patient based on how much money you're going to make off the case," says Mr. Gintis, now a researcher affiliated with the Santa Fe Institute, an interdisciplinary research and education center.

Students should also learn to consider the impact their actions might have on their professions. Says Mr. Gintis: "I don't think people like Skilling would take the chances they did if they thought their peers would view them as rats who were besmirching the image of business."

EVALUATING THE AUTHOR'S ARGUMENTS:

According to this viewpoint, today's business schools are placing shareholder profits ahead of social benefits (building good will by doing what is best for the customer and the community). Based on the arguments in this viewpoint, what are the risks of ignoring social benefits in favor of gaining unethical profits and what are the risks of ignoring profits to increase social benefits?

Corporate Cheating Stems from Misplaced Loyalty

David Callahan

"The likely motives of Sullivan and his accountants were two-fold: a desire to please the boss and an impulse to protect the company."

According to this viewpoint, when Scott Sullivan was Chief Financial Officer (CFO) of WorldCom, he oversaw one of the largest cheating scandals in the history of corporate America—an $11 billion fraud. According to author David Callahan, prior to this, Sullivan had a "stellar reputation in the telecom industry." Just four years before he was arrested for the fraud, *CFO Magazine* awarded Sullivan the CFO Excellence Award. Even when Sullivan was in college, he was reputed to be the "straight-arrow type." According to the author, Sullivan wasn't motivated by greed or selfishness. Sullivan cheated to please his boss and protect the company. David Callahan, a nationally recognized expert on cheating, is author of this viewpoint and the bestselling book, *The Cheating Culture: Why More Americans Are Doing Wrong to Get Ahead.*

AS YOU READ, CONSIDER THE FOLLOWING QUESTIONS:
1. According to the author, when WorldCom was at its height, how much was Scott Sullivan worth?
2. According to this viewpoint, while accountants at WorldCom can't be compared to SS officers, what did WorldCom executives lose in following criminal orders?
3. According to a quote by Sullivan in this viewpoint, what did Sullivan say when he pled guilty to federal charges?

Even though Scott Sullivan admitted last year to overseeing WorldCom's $11 billion fraud—making him easily one of the biggest crooks ever—most business reporters probably wouldn't recognize Sullivan at the table next to theirs. He's pale and nondescript, the way accountants are supposed to be. During the go-go years, he was never known for any exotic hobbies or pithy sayings. Until WorldCom collapsed, and a cuffed Sullivan took a perp walk into a New York courthouse in July 2002, he remained largely anonymous.

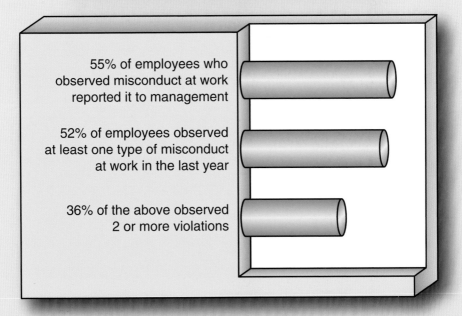

Unethical Conduct in the Workplace

55% of employees who observed misconduct at work reported it to management

52% of employees observed at least one type of misconduct at work in the last year

36% of the above observed 2 or more violations

Taken from: www.ethics.org/research/2005-press-release.asp

Sullivan's background, which I explore in my book, *The Cheating Culture*, fits his bland persona. He grew up in a middle-class household in upstate New York and went to Oswego State University, where he majored in business and accounting. One of his professors later remembered him as a mature, straight-arrow type who had "a unique ability to get along with others." After college, he took a position in Albany with KPMG, one of the nation's biggest accounting firms. Later he moved on to a telecommunications company in South Florida, which later merged with the fast growing WorldCom. Sullivan impressed CEO Ebbers, who promoted him quickly up the ranks and made him CFO in 1994. Sullivan was only 33.

Sullivan Had a Good Reputation

At WorldCom, Sullivan was well-liked and respected. He also had a stellar reputation in the industry at large. Sullivan was seen as even tempered and reasonable, in contrast to a lot of the wild men in the telecom industry, Ebbers included. In 1998, *CFO magazine* gave him its annual CFO Excellence Award. Back in New York, Oswego University profiled him in the alumni magazine—lauding him not just for his business success but for contributing time and money to improve his alma mater.

Sullivan spent the 1990s working closely with Ebbers to build WorldCom into one of the hottest companies in America. Together they wowed Wall Street, took over the long-distance giant MCI, gobbled up a bunch of smaller companies, and rode WorldCom's soaring stock to personal riches. Ebbers and Sullivan were known as an inseparable corporate duo, but privately Sullivan was said to loath his brash boss. And if we believe Sullivan and the government prosecutors,

Sullivan was against Ebbers's plan to lie about company earnings to prop up WorldCom's stock as the telecom bubble collapsed. Likewise, the accountants who worked under Sullivan were deeply upset when they were asked to concoct false numbers.

Good People Do Dishonest Things

So why did they do it? One answer, at least for Sullivan, may have been money. When WorldCom stock was at its height, in early 2000, Sullivan was worth tens of millions on paper. As the company's stock started to sink, this fortune began to evaporate. It would have been a natural impulse for Sullivan to want to stem his losses. Yet if this were the case, then Sullivan should have been an eager participant in Ebbers's plan to cook the books. He wasn't. Also, there is no evidence that the accountants who worked below Sullivan had a major financial stake in WorldCom's stock.

The more likely motives of Sullivan and his accountants were twofold: a desire to please the boss and an impulse to protect the company. The first of these should come as no surprise. One of the grim lessons of the twentieth century—stressed by thinkers such as Hannah Arendt and Stanley Milgram—is that good people in hierarchies do evil things. While the accountants at WorldCom can't be compared to SS officers, their compliance with criminal orders is just the latest example of how ordinary people will kiss their integrity goodbye to be a team player.

People Must Pay for Their Mistakes

The second motive also speaks to the human frailty of individuals caught in a bind. Joseph Wells, a former FBI agent and founder of the Association of Certified Fraud Examiners, said in an interview for my book that a hallmark of high-level fraud is "rationalization, the ability to call the fraud by a nice name." One way to do this is by reinterpreting accounting rules to give a struggling company more breathing space. Top company officials may convince themselves that they are simply looking out for the good of those who work for them. Surely, Scott Sullivan hoped and prayed that WorldCom would get past its rough spot and that the corner cutting along the way would be forgotten. Sullivan said as much when he pled guilty to federal charges last March: "I took these actions, knowing they were wrong, in a misguided effort to preserve the company to allow it to withstand what I believed were temporary financial difficulties."

The reluctance with which Sullivan and his fellow accountants participated in WorldCom's crimes doesn't excuse their actions. Each should still go to prison in order to deter future wrongdoing. Yet their apparent motives suggest a more complex understanding of white-collar crime and underscore the importance of reforms that can change the ethical climate in business. The corporate clean-up of the past few years has focused on such things as making CEOs and board directors more accountable for earnings statements, and on reducing conflicts of interest among auditors and stock analysts. While these steps are important—and, in fact, much tougher reforms are imperative—new rules only scratch at the surface. Also needed are new reflexes toward honesty among corporate employees that are so strong and automatic they can overcome the impulse to follow orders and protect institutional interests.

EVALUATING THE AUTHOR'S ARGUMENTS:

In this viewpoint, misplaced loyalty to the boss and company were at the root of corporate executive cheating. In the previous viewpoint, profits and personal gain were the root cause of corporate executive cheating. Based on what you know from these two viewpoints, does the motive for cheating make a difference in the outcome? Give reasons for your answer.

Chapter 3

What Is the Solution to Cheating?

Varying degrees of cheating make infidelity a troublesome subject for courtrooms.

Spying with New Technology May Curb Infidelity

Andrew G. Marshall

"Evidence that would previously have taken a team of police detectives weeks to gather can now be gathered by an enterprising amateur in a few days."

In this viewpoint, the author explains how cell phones, e-mails, and chat rooms have made relationship cheating easier. However, he points out that new technology has also made it easier to spy and catch the cheater. As a result, two things have changed; "wronged" partners approach cheaters differently and affairs are getting shorter. In the past a wronged partner would suspect, accuse, and gradually gather proof. By the time sufficient evidence was compiled, the affair might have been going on for years. Now, with new technology, a wronged partner gathers proof in a matter of minutes and presents solid evidence at the initial confrontation with the cheater. Therefore, affairs are discovered and reckoned with much more quickly. The author suggests that one way to stop cheating is to redefine the meaning of cheating.

Andrew G. Marshall is a marital therapist of 20 years and regularly contributes to the *Times*. He is author of the book *I Love You But I'm Not In Love With You*.

LOOK

Andrew G. Marshall, "Ringing Changes on Illicit Affairs," *The Times (United Kingdom)*, June 11, 2005, p. 10. Reproduced by permission.

AS YOU READ, CONSIDER THE FOLLOWING QUESTIONS:
1. According to the author, how has the pattern of cheating changed in the last two or three years?
2. In the author's opinion, how has new technology affected the length of illicit affairs?
3. According to a five-year study presented by the author, how do some couples redefine faithfulness?

Changing work patterns and new technology is making it easier than ever before to launch into an affair. With few jobs still nine-to-five, work provides a constant alibi while conferences and training weekends offer cover for lovers to spend nights together. Meanwhile the Internet supplies a multitude of chat rooms to meet new people; Friends Reunited to track down old flames; and even "discreet and confidential" extramarital online dating. Mobile phones and e-mails allow round-the-clock flirting and the scheduling of a last-minute rendezvous. But while starting to cheat might be simple, keeping the affair secret has become almost impossible.

As a relationship counsellor, with 20 years experience, I am familiar with the pain and emotional fallout when an affair is discovered. However, the past two or three years the pattern has changed. In the past the "wronged" partner would probably have suspected something and confronted their other half who would normally deny everything. It was not uncommon for this to happen twice before the cheating was finally uncovered. I would regularly counsel couples where an affair had lasted more than three years. Today, he or she will get proof first and then confront.

Cheaters Are Caught Quickly

There is no shortage of possible "smoking guns". The most common evidence comes from the mobile phone. "David had been very distracted and very short with me," says Julie, who has lived with her partner for eight years. "I put it down to work stress until a friend suggested he might be cheating. I dismissed the idea but it kept eating away at me, and one Sunday morning, when I'd gone down to make breakfast, I saw his phone lying on the table." It took her only a few minutes to open his text message folder and trace his calls. "He had

Private investigators have many high-tech tools at their disposal to catch cheating spouses in the act.

made a pathetic attempt at deceit by calling this girl 'Martin' in his address book—who is an old school friend—but the area code was wrong," she says.

Other people arrive in my counselling session with itemised phone bills that prove how often and for how long their partner has been speaking to the other man or other woman. "She spoke to this guy, who is supposed to be just a friend, five times on her day off. She didn't call me once," says James, a 32-year-old financial services worker. "I had always suspected something, but now I had my ammunition. I threatened to delve further. After 40 minutes of this, I suppose, inter-rogation, she broke down and it came tumbling out."

Other partners go through the history on the home computer and no matter how careful the cheaters are to cover their tracks, they ulti-mately slip up. Credit card bills, shopping receipts and other paper trails generated by modern technology provide unlimited information about our lives. I even had a case where a suspicious husband bribed his wife's firm's security officer to view the CCTV of the office car park. He wanted to check what time she had really left work and saw her kissing a colleague goodbye.

Affairs Are Getting Shorter

Evidence that would previously have taken a team of police detectives weeks of door-to-door inquiries and surveillance can now be gathered by an enterprising amateur in a few days. The result is that the length of affairs has dropped dramatically. In a recent survey at my counselling centre, all new clients were asked why they were seeking help and how long they had had this problem. The most common duration for affairs was less than six months (68 per cent), followed by 6 months to 18 months (25 per cent). Only a handful of affairs had lasted longer and these were most likely to involve older couples less conversant with new technologies.

The chances of being found out are about to climb even more dramatically. Software companies are offering packages that help the computer illiterate to spy on a partner's e-mail account. And phone companies provide a tracking service that logs the location of any mobile phone, as long as it is switched on. . . .

Some People Redefine Cheating

Looking at all the evidence, it seems that the end of the secret affair is in sight. But human nature being what it is, the temptation to stray will still be there. So what is the alternative? One possible future is offered by the experience of the gay community. In a five-year study of 156 gay couples, aged between 20 and 69, in California, the psychologists David McWhirter and Andrew Mattinson found that not one couple who had been together for more than five years was sexually exclusive.

"We are faithful to each other where it counts; in our hearts," said one typical respondent. Each couple had negotiated a set of rules. Most banned having sex with friends and in the "marital" home, while others forbade a repeat performance. The overriding rule was full disclosure. If this approach was adopted by heterosexual couples, we would discover if there was any truth in something I often hear the "innocent" partner say to the "guilty" one: "It's the lying and deception I can't live with."

The other possible future also comes from America: the get-tough approach from Bible-based self-help books. David Clarke, in his book *I Don't Love You Anymore* lays out an action plan based on Matthew XVIII for dealing with cheating spouses. He writes: "This is not a marital problem, it is a sin problem. You try to get the man to stop sinning."

Whichever of these two futures dominates, one thing is certain: the usual British muddle—everybody signing up to fidelity but most of us straying at some point—is no longer tenable.

EVALUATING THE AUTHOR'S ARGUMENTS:

In this viewpoint, the author states that new technology makes it nearly impossible to hide cheating. However, getting caught does not necessarily remove the temptation to cheat in the future. One alternative, presented by the author, is for couples to surrender to the human tendency to stray and negotiate new rules that allow for some outside affairs. In your opinion, how might these "new rules" affect the level of trust within a marriage? Also, do you think "new rules" would cause an increase or a decrease in spousal spying with new technology? Please give reasons for your answers.

Spying with New Technology Is Not an Ethical Solution to Cheating

Camille Calman

"Some reasonable expectation of privacy remains within a marriage, and spousal spying by surveillance software violates that expectation."

Author Camille Calman argues that while it is not currently illegal to use surveillance software to spy on spouses, it is a violation of communication privacy and trust that is expected in a marriage. Calman argues that current law that addresses spousal spying with new technology—surveillance software—is inconsistent with existing law banning spousal spying with old technology, such as wiretapping. Furthermore, the author states that conditions such as joint ownership of a computer by marriage mates or protection by passwords does not justify the current loophole that allows for new technology spying on spouses. Camille Calman received a J.D. degree from Columbia Law School in 2006 and currently practices law with Debevoise & Plimpton LLP in New York.

Camille Calman, "Spy vs. Spouse: Regulating Surveillance Software on Shared Marital Computers," *Columbia Law Review*, vol. 105, October 31, 2005, pp. 2097-2100, 2113-2115, 2121-2123 and 2134. Copyright © 2007 by the *Columbia Law Review*. All rights reserved. Reproduced by permission.

AS YOU READ, CONSIDER THE FOLLOWING QUESTIONS:
1. According to this viewpoint, regulation of surveillance software is necessary for what two reasons?
2. From the author's point of view, what is one of the most important aspects of personal autonomy?
3. According to this viewpoint, some courts have found an expectation of privacy in shared computers as long as the information is protected by what means?

Married individuals who share computers with their spouses may be sharing more information than they anticipate. Thanks to the invention of surveillance software, anyone with suspicions about his or her spouse's computer activities now has an inexpensive and technologically simple way to monitor every keystroke—every e-mail, every instant message, every document written, every website visited. Information formerly hidden from all but the most technologically advanced computer user is now readily available to anyone with $69.95 to spare.

Although installing software on someone else's computer without permission can be tortious [an act for which a person may be sued for damages] and even criminal, installing software on a computer one owns jointly with someone else is perfectly legal under federal and state law—though certainly morally questionable when done surreptitiously [secretly]. Because of the joint ownership issue, current wiretapping and privacy law do not prohibit, or provide a remedy for, this form of interspousal spying. The statutory framework covering wiretapping and other invasions of privacy protects spouses from similar intrusions using older technologies, but marital use of surveillance software falls through a loophole.

Surveillance Software Should Be Regulated

This note argues that states should close that loophole with new statutes regulating the use of surveillance software. Such statutes would primarily affect married couples because they are the chief users of the software and are also the individuals most likely to share ownership of a computer. Regulation is necessary for two reasons: to protect privacy rights of married individuals in personal communications, and to reinforce the social perception of marriage as a partnership based on trust. . . .

Consumers can choose from hundreds of surveillance software programs, some for sale commercially and others available for download at no cost. The best-known commercial manufacturer is SpectorSoft, which in 1999 began marketing its Spector "screen shot" software as a tool for parents to monitor their children's Internet use. The company's president decided "on a lark" to run advertisements suggesting that the software could also keep an eye on cheating spouses, and sales, formerly lackluster, increased approximately tenfold. By 2002, more than forty percent of the program's purchasers were using the program to spy on spouses, while under one-third were using it to monitor their children. Since the mid-1990s, when surveillance software was first marketed, divorce lawyers have observed rising use of such products among divorcing couples. . . .

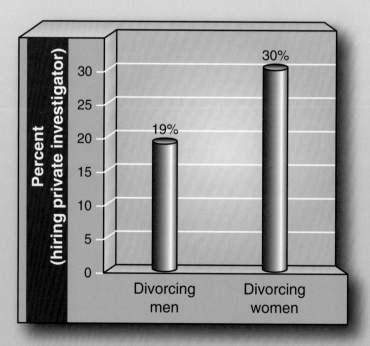

Taken from: "Sorry Affair is Good News for Private Eyes,"
The Times (UK), April 23, 2007.

Married People Have Privacy Rights

Until the nineteenth century, the law considered a married couple to be a single legal entity in which the wife, subordinated to her husband, had no right to own property, enter into contracts, or control her own earnings. The legal doctrine . . . dictated that a woman, on marrying, gave up all such rights to her husband. In such a relationship, it would be unthinkable for spouses to have privacy rights from one another. However, the passage of the Married Women's Property Acts by various states in the nineteenth century and more recent changes in the status of women and in divorce laws have led gradually to more modern conceptions of marriage. While there is no one monolithic [single] vision of modern marriage, the fact that women are no longer required by U.S. law to give up property or autonomous powers of decision-making when they enter into the married state means that marriage today inevitably looks more like a partnership of individuals who retain important individual rights.

Changes in privacy law and in social constructs of marriage converge in the area of communications privacy. One of the most important aspects of personal autonomy is freedom to communicate with other persons. The law does not require married couples to tell each other everything; such a requirement could not be practically enforced. Entry into marriage does not entail signing away the right to communicate privately with persons outside the marital relationship. Some writers have described spheres or zones of privacy, with an innermost zone open to no one, and the next zone open only to spouses, close friends, and relatives. Even within those inner spheres, the law does—and should—recognize a right of personal privacy.

Married People Have Limited Privacy

Certainly individuals within a marriage have far more access to each other's private information than strangers would. Spouses can behave in many ways that are intrusive but not legally actionable: They can

The American public has speculated for years about alleged infidelities committed by President John F. Kennedy during his marriage to Jacqueline Lee Bouvier.

read letters or e-mails or credit card bills that their spouses have already opened; they can eavesdrop on live conversations; they can rummage through filing cabinets; they can read diaries. But the use of electronic devices to spy at times and in places where live eavesdropping is impossible—to eavesdrop in a way that evades the likelihood of detection—seems to cross a line.

A person's right to privacy is not absolute and must be weighed against countervailing rights and social interests. Clearly the expectation of privacy is lower within a marriage than in other less intimate relationships. Some reasonable expectation of privacy remains, however, and spousal spying by surveillance software violates that expectation. . . .

A lowered expectation of privacy on computers that are shared also cannot justify the use of surveillance software by spouses. Some courts have held that there is no reasonable expectation of privacy at all on a co-owned or shared computer since both parties have consented to access by the other. But this theory leads to an unjust outcome in the case of surveillance software: The couple that can purchase two computers and deny each other access receives greater privacy protection than the couple that can afford only one. Such a regime falsely implies that privacy is a luxury available to the wealthy rather than a right belonging to all.

Some courts have found an expectation of privacy on shared computers as long as the information in question is password protected. Password protection might serve as presumptive evidence of an intent to maintain privacy. Surveillance software would thus be at least a partial invasion of privacy, since it records indiscriminately, without regard to password protection. But unsophisticated computer users might not be sufficiently aware of what material the password protects. The law should not protect the technologically savvy user more completely than the novice.

Spousal Surveillance Differs from Employer Surveillance

Courts have found that employees have little or no expectation of privacy regarding e-mails on workplace computers. An employee's privacy is trumped by the recognition that an employer should be able to monitor its resources, both human and electronic. However, a similar rationale cannot justify spying at home, since the computer is shared marital property, and the spying spouse does not "own" the other spouse's time in the way an employer "owns" an employee's time.

Spousal spying using surveillance software cannot be justified on the basis of any lowered expectation of privacy. Communications privacy is a value our society recognizes and protects, at least for adults in private places such as the home. We ought to protect such privacy with a consistent legal framework. Therefore, individuals need some legal recourse when they are the victims of spousal spying. . . .

New Laws Are Needed

[In conclusion] surveillance software creates an invasion of privacy every bit as objectionable as wiretapping or the opening of postal mail. Such intrusions should be regulated, not just to bring consistency to the law of communications privacy, but to sustain a vision of marriage as a partnership of autonomous individuals, characterized by mutual trust.

EVALUATING THE AUTHOR'S ARGUMENTS:

In this viewpoint, Camille Calman argues that spousal spying with new technology may be legal, but it is a poor choice as it erodes the mutual trust expected in a marriage. In contrast, the previous viewpoint author, Andrew G. Marshall, argues that spousal spying with new technology saves time and money for the innocent partner when cheating is suspected. It also allows the couple to face the problem more quickly. Based on the arguments in these two viewpoints, do you think that spousal spying with new technology enhances or erodes mutual trust in a marriage? Cite reasons for your answer.

The Honor Code Is Not a Good Solution to Cheating

Miguel Roig and Amanda Marks

> *"Merely creating an honor code and handing it to the students will not be sufficient to curb the current increase of academic dishonesty."*

According to this viewpoint, in 2004 a large, private university with approximately 20,000 students decided to implement an honor code. This presented an opportunity to study the effects of the honor code by surveying students before and after the implementation. Authors and researchers, Miguel Roig and Amanda Marks, did that and wrote about it in this viewpoint. It is important to note that freshmen students were surveyed, as the new honor code was limited to this group the first year. The initial student survey took place before the honor code was implemented. A second survey took place after the honor code was adopted and promoted by the following means: online in the Office of the Provost's Web page, on paper when copies were distributed at "Freshman Orientation", verbally at the new student convocation, again by printed page at a university fair, and finally, in classroom discussion. According to this

Miguel Roig and Amanda Marks, "Attitudes Toward Cheating Before and After the Implementation of a Modified Honor Code: A Case Study," *Ethics & Behavior,* vol. 16, April 2006, pp. 163-5, 169-70. Copyright © 2006 Lawrence Erlbaum Associates, Inc. Reproduced by permission of the Taylor & Francis Group, LLC, www.informaworld.com, and the authors.

viewpoint, despite all of this effort, the study found that the new honor code had very little impact on students' attitude toward cheating (ATC). Miguel Roig and Amanda Marks, from the Department of Psychology at the Notre Dame Division of St. John's College, authored this study and the article from which it was taken.

AS YOU READ, CONSIDER THE FOLLOWING QUESTIONS:

1. According to the authors, by examining student's attitudes immediately after the implementation of the honor code, what could be determined?
2. According to the authors, it could be argued that the absence of differences in the ATC (attitudes toward cheating) scores between samples may have stemmed from what?
3. The findings reported in this study, along with data from other recent studies, suggest what kind of progress regarding curbing of cheating?

Growing evidence reported by [Don] McCabe [Founding President of the Center for Academic Integrity] and his colleagues indicates that the incidence of cheating is lower in colleges and universities that have an academic honor code relative to those that lack such codes. McCabe interpreted this evidence as suggesting that the presence of an honor code enhances the climate of academic integrity in these institutions. That is, entering students who are made keenly aware that they are now functioning within an academic code of honor are thought to internalize these principles, thereby reducing their propensity to engage in academically dishonest acts. More important, students who perceive that their peers are reluctant to cheat are themselves less likely to engage in such behaviors, and therefore, a culture of integrity is established. Because in recent years cheating has been increasingly perceived as a significant problem at many schools, a number of colleges and universities have begun to implement academic honor codes.

McCabe and others grouped academic honor codes into two basic types: traditional honor codes and modified honor codes. *Traditional honor codes* are characterized by a written pledge of academic honesty, a

The honor code is strongly enforced in military academies, but it is harder to encourage general population students to follow the code.

student–faculty judiciary structure for handling honor code violations, peer reporting of academically dishonest activities, and unproctored exams. *Modified honor codes* generally consist of a written pledge and some form of judiciary structure for honor code violations.

A New Study Was Needed

Little research exists into differences in academic dishonesty between traditional versus modified honor code institutions. One recent large-scale study by McCabe et al. (2002), however, suggested that there is less cheating in schools with traditional honor codes than in schools with modified honor codes. In turn, cheating appears to occur with less frequency in schools with a modified honor code than in those with no honor code.

One concern with the available literature is that the findings are largely based on comparisons of self-reported cheating from students across institutions that either have had an honor code for some time or lack one. Such a research strategy makes it difficult to rule out the possibility that the student bodies at these institutions differ along other relevant dimensions, giving rise to the observed differences in cheating.

A Favorable Opportunity Presented Itself

This study was carried out, in part, to address the previous concern by taking advantage of one institution's plan to implement an academic honor code. Thus, we were able to collect data immediately before and after the implementation of the honor code. We chose to examine student attitudes toward cheating for two reasons. First, we felt that by examining students' attitudes immediately after the implementation of an honor code, we could determine the extent to which students' assimilation of the code affected their attitudes toward academically dishonest behaviors before a period of time that, in our view, offers the greatest temptations to engage in the actual cheating behaviors: final examinations. Although we acknowledge that the relationship between behavior and its underlying attitudes is not always consistent, there is some evidence that, in the case of academic dishonesty, students' favorable attitudes toward cheating are a good measure of their likelihood of engaging in such activities.

A second reason for focusing on attitudes is that one of us had earlier carried out a study on students' and professors' attitudes toward cheating, and therefore, we felt that the earlier data would give us a better perspective from which we could better interpret data from this study. In that study, we had found that students' attitudes toward cheating were much more tolerant than the attitudes held by professors. In addition, we found that the attitudes that students ascribed to their professors were similar to the attitudes that professors themselves reported to have.

Researchers Predicted a Change In Student Attitude

On learning of the institution's intentions to implement a modified honor code, we obtained a sample of students attitudes toward cheating [ATC] during the semester prior to the implementation of the honor code. The honor code was introduced during the fall of 2004, but only the entering first-year students were introduced to the code. We therefore sampled a group of first-year students and asked them to complete the same questionnaires. In view of the evidence presented by McCabe and other available evidence, we hypothesized that students who were exposed to the honor code would report stronger conservative attitudes toward cheating than would those who had not been exposed to the honor code. We also predicted that honor code students, relative to their non-honor code counterparts, would also believe that professors would hold less tolerant attitudes toward cheating. . . .

The Honor Code Had Little Impact

The data clearly show[ed that] there was virtually no difference in ATC scores between the sample that completed the questionnaires before the implementation of the institution's honor code and the sample that completed it afterwards. . . .

As McCabe and [researcher Linda Klebe] Treviño (2002) pointed out, honor codes are not very meaningful unless students are continually made aware of them and are exposed to ongoing dialogues in the class and outside of class about relevant matters of integrity and honor. . . .

Another important factor that may have played a role in our findings is that although only 20% of undergraduates are considered part-time students, the institution studied is characterized as an urban, "commuter" school. McCabe and Treviño (2002) pointed out that honor codes may not be as effective in schools where large numbers of students attend school part time and/or live off campus.

Most Students Were Uninvolved

It could be argued that the absence of differences in ATC scores between the sample may have stemmed from a general awareness on the part of students who completed the questionnaires prior to the establishment of the honor code that the university community was concerned about the problem of cheating and that an honor code was about to be instituted. Very few students, however, took an active part

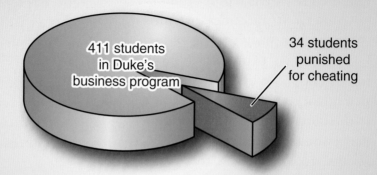

May 2007: Largest Cheating Scandal in History of Duke University

411 students in Duke's business program

34 students punished for cheating

Taken from: Martha Waggoner, "Duke Biz School Punishes 34 for Cheating," Associated Press, May 2, 2007.

in initial meetings and/or were part of the process throughout the formulation of the honor code. More important, a review of Table 2 shows that the means for students' self-reported attitudes toward cheating and those they ascribe to college professors are very similar to, if not slightly more tolerant (lower) than, the corresponding data obtained over a decade using the very same questionnaire (i.e., ATC). These comparisons point to the more plausible explanation that the honor code, as implemented by the institution, simply did not have any immediate effect on students attitudes.

More Involvement May Be Key

It remains to be seen whether additional efforts at promulgating the honor code will have the expected effects of changing students' attitudes and overall academic integrity climate of the institution. McCabe and Treviño (2002) described several such strategies involving both faculty and administrators, and researcher R. L. Dufresne (2004) strongly argued for the active involvement of all members of the community, including students, in formulating and upholding the honor code. . . .

The findings reported in this study, along with the data from other recent studies on academic dishonesty, suggest that, in spite of all the research and media attention devoted to the problem of cheating within the past 10 to 15 years, little if any significant progress appears to have been made in abating this troublesome issue. We believe that the creation and implementation of honor codes represent a step in the right direction. However, merely creating an honor code and handing it to students will not be sufficient to curb the current incidence of academic dishonesty, for students' attitudes remain far too favorable with respect to cheating, and such pervasive views represent a significant negative contribution to the academic integrity climate of an institution.

EVALUATING THE AUTHORS' ARGUMENTS:

In this viewpoint, the authors noted that though the new honor code was given to the students in many different ways—online, in print, and verbally—it was virtually ineffective in changing student ATC (attitudes toward cheating). At the same time, the authors stated that "very few students took an active part in the initial meetings and/ or...the formulation of the honor code." Based on what you learned in this viewpoint and what you know about academic cheating, do you think that the honor code would have a greater impact if it were student driven? Give reasons for your answer.

The Honor Code Is an Effective Deterrent to Cheating

Shirley T. Fleischmann

"We recognize that students will progress in their understanding and acceptance of the Honor Concept; nonetheless, the signing of the pledge of understanding makes it clear that the Honor Concept is not optional."

According to the author, Professor Shirley T. Fleischmann, Grand Valley State University's School of Engineering has an Honor Code that promotes not only academic honor, but honor as a way of life. Patterned after the United States Military Academy of West Point, Fleischmann points out that Grand Valley creates a culture of honor that runs counter to the predominate culture in America. To create this culture, students are given a laminated wallet card with the honor code and an explanation of why integrity is a professional requirement; students sign a pledge and are expected to develop a high level of integrity, competence, courage, and compassion; and the school's seal is inscribed with these values. As part of the curriculum, students regularly identify ethical dilemmas and discuss ways to resolve them. According to Fleischmann, the education process is sealed at graduation with the Iron Ring Ceremony in which each student

Shirley T. Fleischmann, "Teaching Ethics: More Than An Honor Code," *Science and Engineering Ethics,* vol. 12, 2006, pp. 382, 385-89. Reproduced by permission of the publisher and the author.

has a stainless steel pinky ring put on his or her finger as a reminder that honor is a lifetime commitment. Shirley T. Fleischmann is a professor of mechanical engineering at Grand Valley State University and author of the article from which this viewpoint was taken.

AS YOU READ, CONSIDER THE FOLLOWING QUESTIONS:
1. According to this viewpoint, the cultural shift that has accompanied the technical change has affected the principles by which we live in what way?
2. According to the book *When Hope and Fear Collide,* cited in this viewpoint, undergraduate students need an education that provides what four things?
3. According to this viewpoint, at West Point cadets receive a laminated wallet card with what printed on it?

A n honor code involves a shared set of values. While the general culture 40 years ago still supported the idea of living under a shared set of values, the general culture today does not support such an idea. It is critical for educators to realize that our surrounding culture has moved away from the idea of a shared ethics standard and the moral absolutes that form the basis for an honor code. . . .

It might be tempting to say that the rapid change over the past 20 years is the source of our difficulty in teaching ethics, but technology is mostly a matter of devising new and better tools. There is no need to abandon the principles by which we live just because our tools have changed.

Current Culture Does Not Value Honor

But the cultural shift that has accompanied this technological change has affected the general understanding of the principles by which we live; in fact it encourages abandoning those principles and moving toward a culture rooted only in the present and without standards for excellence and honorable living. As educators we must understand the nature of this cultural shift before we can design effective curriculums that will draw students in, help them break away from the harmful aspects of the culture that surrounds them, and encourage them to

Honor Code Deters Cheating

Survey results of 35 college students who attended a college without an Honor Code, and then experienced the Honor Code in one class.

Item	Percent Yes
Have experienced honor code before	22.9%
Honor code affected thoughts and/or behavior	51.4%
Have cheated in college	42.9%
Have cheated in another psychology class	25.7%
Tempted to cheat in this class	17.1%
Cheated in this class	5.7%
Witnessed cheating in college	60.0%
Witnessed cheating in another psychology class	40.0%
Witnessed cheating in this class	11.4%
Believe others may have cheated in this class	57.1%

Taken from: Yasmine L. Konheim-Kalkstein, "Use of Classroom Honor Code in Higher Education," The Journal of Credibility Assessment and Witness Psychology (Boise State University), 2006.

embrace the idea of living with honor in a culture that often does not understand or value it. . . .

In his pamphlet *Six Steps for Remedying Contemporary Ethical Problems,* Robert Spitzer asks, "How is it that Enron, WorldCom, Arthur Anderson, and so many other firms of supposed high integrity found themselves in complete ethical and commercial dissolution?. . . How did the 80s lead to our second millennial problems?" Three of the four cultural conditions to which he attributes these problems are: (1) the move from principle-based to utilitarian criteria, (2) the decline of traditional principle-based instruction, (3) the complexity and rapidity of decisionmaking and the failure to integrate ethical reflection into it.

Honor Can Be Taught

Spitzer offers specific steps for redressing the problem: exercising leadership from the top, forming ethical communities, defining inviolable principles, asking the right questions during the decision-making process, and a mechanism for responding to questions. These items provide specific guidance for curriculum design.

Further curriculum design guidance is offered by Levine and Cureton in a book entitled *When Hope and Fear Collide: A Portrait of Today's College Student* In reviewing studies of college students from the late 1970s through the 1990s, Levine noted a sudden and dramatic change (like flipping a light switch) in the attitudes, values, and beliefs of typical undergraduates in the 1990s. Unlike the pessimistic students of the 1980s, students were typically optimistic about their futures; but they were also afraid because to them things seemed to be falling apart—hence the title of the book, *When Hope and Fear Collide.* The book details their findings, and at the end Levine and Cureton state that current undergraduates need an education that provides them with the following four things:

Hope—the kind of hope that helps students hold on to their dreams.

Responsibility—many of today's students feel that they must choose between security and responsibility, because it is not possible to do good and to do well.

Appreciation of differences—a difficult topic for today's students

Efficacy—a sense that one can make a difference. . . .

Are there any other resources for curriculum planning that can help us bring about such a momentous change? In fact, we do have a guide—an engineering school with a 200-year-long record of success: the United States Military Academy at West Point. It is difficult to think of a more radical change than the transition from civilian to military life. . . .

It is worth looking for the features that can be duplicated because the task of transforming incoming students into trustworthy professionals is similar in many ways to the task that West Point faces. . . .

West Point Leads the Way

At West Point, cadets receive a laminated card with the honor code on one side and three rules of thumb (similar to Father Spitzer's "asking the right questions") on the other side. This occurs as part of the induction day process, along with haircuts, issuing of uniforms, and the first experience of reporting to a superior officer. At Grand Valley we also give our students a laminated card on which is printed the Honor Code, three rules of thumb, and a short explanation of why integrity is a professional requirement. Like West Point, we make a special event of it—an Honor Concept orientation at which we welcome the students to the School of Engineering and to the engineering profession. . . .

Students are asked to carry the card in their wallets. Our experience has been that they value having this concrete reminder of their choice to live with honor. The entire Honor Concept orientation is a clear signal to our students that they are entering a professional community that will function as an ethical community and live by clearly defined inviolable principles. . . .

West Point does not hesitate to tell cadets which character traits they expect they will develop. Similarly, we have identified four character traits (or virtues) that we expect our students to develop to a high degree: integrity and competence (related to the intellect), and courage and compassion (related to the heart). These virtues appear on the school seal, and students are provided with a handout summarizing how we define each virtue and how it is related to excellence in engineering. The seal is another artifact, something that our students can use to say: *This is who I am, this is what I stand for.* It has been our experience that students are enthusiastic about displaying the seal on report covers, project posters, and other work.

FAST FACT

A 1995 study found that 71% of students that do not have an honor code have cheated.

Timing Is Critical

The timing of this introduction to the Honor Code and the Honor Concept as a way of life is important. It must occur at the very beginning of a student's academic career. Like the service academies, we do not expect that our students will make an instant change. We recognize that students will progress in their understanding and acceptance of the Honor Concept; nonetheless, the signing of the pledge of understanding makes it clear that the Honor Concept is not optional.

We put the Honor Code and Honor Concept to use early in the first year by taking time out of the freshman design class as soon as the students are beginning to experience academic pressure. We present

Pep rallies are encouraging students to live ethical and trustworthy lives.

them with a case study about a student who is tempted to violate the code of ethics, and in analyzing the case we illustrate the use of the rules of thumb. . . .

Many Encounters Are Necessary

Whenever possible, students are presented with opportunities to exercise the Honor Concept. For example, honesty in the presentation of homework is regularly presented as an honor concept issue. It does not hurt to remind students of this on a regular basis. Some students may be tempted to cheat; it is important to acknowledge this and then to restate the expectation that they will follow the rules. . . .

The way we end the undergraduate experience is as important as the way we begin it. At West Point there is an impressive graduation and commissioning exercise, followed by a ceremony in which the insignia of rank is pinned to the new uniform. At Grand Valley, engineering students finish at the end of the summer. We hold a day-long event in which senior projects are highlighted. Industry representatives and families and friends are invited to participate in the events of the day. In the evening we hold the Iron Ring ceremony. This includes a recitation of an honor pledge and the placement of a stainless steel ring on the little finger of the graduate's working hand as a symbol of the pledge. This is our commissioning and pinning ceremony. It is a fitting celebration of accomplishment with a lasting reminder of the graduate's commitment to live with honor as he or she begins a professional career in engineering. . . .

Only when students embrace the idea of an honor concept as a way of life and allow their educational experiences to transform their sense of themselves is our educational purpose achieved.

In this viewpoint, leadership from the top—as modeled by the West Point Honor Code—is credited with creating a culture of honor at Grand Valley State University. According to the author, this culture aims higher than academic honor; it aims for honor as a way of life. It aims to transform students into trustworthy professionals for their lifetime. In contrast, the previous viewpoint suggested that honor codes generally address academic honor and they might be more effective when they are student-driven (when students are involved in creating and promoting the policy). In your opinion, based on these two viewpoints, what do you believe are three key components to an honor code that effectively deters academic cheating? Explain your answer.

Facts About Cheating

Cheating at School

According to the National Education Association:

- 80 percent of surveyed high school students admit to cheating.
- 95 percent of cheating students say they don't get caught.
- 77 percent of cheating students say cheating is not a serious offense.
- 15 percent of surveyed high school students have turned in a paper they bought or downloaded from the Internet.
- 34 percent of surveyed students say their parents don't talk to them about cheating.
- 50 percent of cheating students have used the Internet to plagiarize.
- 33 percent of schools investigated show evidence of cheating on standardized tests, with charter schools being four times as likely to be found cheating as public schools.
- 100 percent of surveyed teachers have caught student cheaters.
- Many students plagiarize unintentionally. In the age of information-sharing, boundaries can become foggy.

Sports Cheating (doping)

According to the National Institute on Drug Abuse:

- Anabolic steroids are synthetic versions of testosterone—the male sex hormone—and they are a controlled substance. Medicinally, they treat body wasting diseases. Illegally, they are used as performance-enhancing drugs.
- To create the performance-enhancing effect, steroids are taken in doses 10 to 100 times the medicinal dose.
- Severe health risks related to steroid use include heart attacks, strokes, liver tumors, kidney failure, and serious psychiatric problems.
- Steroids can be taken orally, by injection, or as an ointment rubbed on the skin.
- "Stacking" refers to abusers taking two or more different anabolic

steroids together in the belief that they have a greater affect on muscle size.

- Withdrawal symptoms from steroids include mood swings, fatigue, restlessness, loss of appetite, insomnia, depression, reduced sex drive, and steroid craving.
- Sports Medicine Research and Testing Laboratory (SMRTL)—one of two drug testing facilities accredited by the World Anti-doping Agency—can detect one-billionth of a gram of steroids in an athlete's blood or urine sample.

Relationship Cheating

According to information gathered on WomanSavers.com:

- 30 percent of people polled feel that sending flirty text messages is cheating.
- 56 percent of people say sexy phone conversations are cheating.
- 75 percent of married women said that it is cheating if her husband kisses another woman romantically.
- 43 percent of married women said it is cheating if her husband holds hands with another woman.
- 38 percent of married women said it is cheating if her husband flirts with another woman.
- 46 percent of men believe that an online affair constitutes adultery.

Additional Cheating Facts

- 90 percent of Americans believe adultery is immoral.
- About 60 percent of men and 40 percent of women will have an affair during the course of their marriage.
- One-third of all divorces are caused by online affairs.
- About 10 percent of Internet users become hooked on cybersex.
- Over 80 percent of men and women regularly flirt with the opposite sex.
- Most people who cheat, cheat with their friends or co-workers.
- 70 percent of all couples stay together after an affair.
- 25 percent of men who cheat say it wasn't worth it.
- 70 percent of people surveyed say that cheating is more socially acceptable now than it was 20 years ago.

Organizations to Contact

The editors have compiled the following list of organizations concerned with the issues debated in this book. The descriptions are derived from materials provided by the organizations. All have publications or information available for interested readers. The list was compiled on the date of publication of the present volume; the information provided here may change. Be aware that many organizations take several weeks or longer to respond to inquiries, so allow as much time as possible.

Aspen Institute

One Dupont Circle, NW, Suite 700, Washington, DC 20036-1133
(202) 736-5800 • fax: (202) 467-0790
e-mail: info@aspenbsp.org • Web site: www.aspeninstitute.org
Aspen Institute, an international nonprofit organization, was founded in 1950 to foster enlightened leadership and open-minded dialogue. Its primary goal is to reconnect people with their values, in business and in all areas of life. Aspen Institute has a wide array of links and free resources available for download.

Canadian Centre for Ethics and Corporate Policy

One Yonge Street, Suite 1801,Toronto, ON ,M5E 1W7
(416) 368-7525 •fax: (416) 369-0515
e-mail: hmyj@ethicscentre.ca • Web site: www.ethicscentre.ca
The centre includes corporations and individuals dedicated to developing and maintaining an ethical corporate culture. It supports research into issues concerning corporate ethics and sponsors seminars, conferences, and lectures on business ethics. It publishes the bimonthly newsletter *Management Ethics.*

Center for Applied Christian Ethics (CACE)

Wheaton College, Wheaton, IL 60187
(630) 752-5886 • fax: (630) 752-5731
e-mail: cace@wheaton.edu • Web site: www.christianethics.org

CACE's goal is to raise moral awareness and elicit moral thinking by encouraging the application of Christian ethics to public policy and personal practice. The center sponsors conferences, workshops, and public debates on ethical issues. It produces a variety of resource materials, including cassettes, videotapes, the triannual newsletter *Discernment,* and the booklet "The Bible, Ethics, and Health Care: Theological Foundations for a Christian Perspective on Health Care."

Center for Business Ethics (CBE)

Adamian Graduate Center, Room 108, Bentley College, Waltham, MA 02452
(781) 891-2981 • fax: (781) 891-2988
e-mail: cbeinfo@bentley.edu • Web site: www.bentley.edu/cbe/
CBE is dedicated to promoting ethical business conduct in contemporary society. It helps corporations and other organizations strengthen their ethical cultures through educational programming and consulting. The center maintains a multimedia library and publishes the quarterly journal *Business and Society Review.* CBE also publishes a variety of books, including *Business Ethics: A Primer* and *Ethics Matters: How to Implement Values-Driven Management.*

Center for Ethics Studies

Marquette University
Academic Support Facility 336, Milwaukee, WI 53233
(414) 288-5824
e-mail: ethics@marquette.edu • Web site: www.marquette.edu/ethics/
Marquette University is a Jesuit institution committed to developing citizens who appreciate the role of values and ethics in their lives. The center's primary goal is to be an ethics resource for the university and the community at large. The center sponsors speakers and programs that focus on issues such as the moral use of police power, in vitro fertilization, and the ethics of health care. The center, a clearinghouse for ethics information, publishes a volume of essays titled *Ethics Across the Curriculum,* a periodic newsletter, and pertinent lectures.

Character Counts!

9841 Airport Blvd. #300, Los Angeles, CA 90045
(310) 846-4800 or (800) 711-2670 • fax: (310) 846-4858
Web site: www.charactercounts.org
Character Counts! was established in 1993 by Josephson Institute to advance the six pillars of character—trustworthiness, respect, responsibility, fairness, caring, and citizenship. The coalition has thousands of members. The center is a resource of free and available for purchase information.

Citizen Works

P O Box 18478, Washington, DC 20036
(202) 265-6164 • fax: (202) 265-0182
e-mail: info@citizenworks.org • Web site: www.citizenworks.org
Citizen Works was founded by Ralph Nader in 2001 to advance justice by strengthening citizen participation in power. A primary goal of this organization is to share information. Press releases such as *Citizen Works Shines a Light on Corporate Tax Avoidance* are available, along with other resources.

Common Cause

1133 19th Street NW, 9th floor, Washington, DC 20036
(202) 833-1200 • fax: (202) 659-3716
e-mail: grassroots@commoncause.org • Web site: www.commoncause
org
Common Cause is a liberal lobbying organization that works to improve the ethical standards of Congress and government in general. Its priorities include campaign reform, making government officials accountable for their actions, and promoting civil rights for all citizens. The organization publishes the quarterly magazine *Common Cause* in addition to position papers and reports.

Ethics Resource Center

1747 Pennsylvania Ave. NW, Suite 400, Washington, DC 20006
(202) 737-2258 • fax: (202) 737-2227
e-mail: ethics@ethics.org • Web site: www.ethics.org
The center works to restore America's ethical foundations by fostering integrity, ethical conduct, and basic values in the nation's institutions.

It also strives to create international coalitions dedicated to global ethics. The center supports character education and has developed several video-based learning programs for use in schools. Its publications include *Creating a Workable Company Code of Ethics, The Desktop Guide to Total Ethics Management,* and the quarterly newsletter *Ethics Today.*

The Hastings Center

21 Malcolm Gordon Road, Garrison, NY 10524-4125
(845) 424-4040 • fax: (845) 424-4545
e-mail: mail@thehastingscenter.org •Web site: www.thehastingscenter.org
Since its founding in 1969, the center has played a central role in responding to advances in medicine, the biological sciences, and the social sciences by raising ethical questions related to such advances. It conducts research on ethical issues and maintains a library of resources relating to ethics. The center publishes books, papers, guidelines, and the bimonthly *Hastings Center Report.*

Institute for Global Ethics

11 Main St., PO Box 563, Camden, ME 04843
(207) 236-6658 • fax: (207) 236-4014
e-mail: webethics@globalethics.org • Web site: http://www.globalethics.org
Dedicated to fostering global ethics, the institute focuses on ethical activities in education, the corporate sector, and public policy. It conducts ethics training seminars, sponsors lectures and workshops, develops curricular materials for elementary and secondary schools, and promotes community-based character education programs. Its publications include the quarterly newsletter *Insights on Global Ethics* and the books *How Good People Make Tough Choices: Resolving the Dilemmas of Ethical Living* and *Heartland Ethics: Voices from the American Midwest.*

Josephson Institute of Ethics

9841 Airport Blvd., #300, Los Angeles, CA 90045
(310) 846-4800 • fax: (310) 846-4857
Web site: www.josephsoninstitute.org
The institute's mission is to improve the ethical quality of society by advocating principled reasoning and ethical decision making. It offers Ethics in the Workplace training seminars as well as specialized consulting services for businesses. Its Character Counts! coalition promotes character education through the partnership of educational and human-service organizations. The institute publishes the book *Good Ideas to Help Young People Develop Good Character,* the booklet "Making Ethical Decisions," and the videotapes *Kids for Character* and *Choices Count!*

Kegley Institute of Ethics

California State University
9001 Stockdale Highway, Bakersfield, CA 93311-1099
(805) 664-3149
e-mail: cmyers@csyb.edu • Web site: www.csubak.edu/kie/IQ.htx
The Kegley Institute is a nonprofit group dedicated to enhancing society's understanding of and ability to respond to contemporary ethical dilemmas. It sponsors conferences and lectures on a wide range of topics, including ethics in journalism, the environment, health care, and business. The institute has published books on technology and ethics and ethics in journalism as well as articles on the death penalty, mental health, fetal rights, and abortion.

Kennedy Institute of Ethics

Georgetown University, Box 571212, Washington, DC 20057-1212
(202) 687-8099 • fax: (202) 687-8089
e-mail: kicourse@gunet.georgetown.edu • Web site: www.georgetown.edu/research/kie
The institute is a teaching and research center that offers ethical perspectives on major policy issues in the fields of medicine, religion, law, journalism, international affairs, and business. It houses the National Reference Center for Bioethics Literature, produces an online medical ethics database, and conducts regular seminars and courses in bio-

ethics. The institute's publications include the annual *Bibliography of Bioethics,* the quarterly *Kennedy Institute of Ethics Journal,* and the Scope Note Series on specific topics concerning biomedical ethics.

National Institute on Drug Abuse (NIDA)

6001 Executive Blvd., Bethesda, MD 20892-9561
(301) 443-1124
e-mail: information@nida.nih.gov •Web site: www.steroidabuse.org
or www.nida.nih.gov
The National Institute on Drug Abuse (NIDA) has a dedicated Web site (www.steroidabuse.org) designed to educate and alert the public to the dangers of anabolic steroids. This site is geared to students, parents, coaches and teachers and has publications, links, and research documents, such as, *Anabolic Steroid Abuse,* available for download or in print.

Turnitin

IParadigms, LLC
1624 Franklin Street, 7th Floor, Oakland, CA 94612
e-mail: info@turnitin.com •Web site: www.turnitin.com
Turnitin was created by by iParadigms, LLC. to detect plagiarism by students. The site is designed not only to catch cheaters, but more importantly, to educate students and teachers alike on how to avoid plagiarism. Some free resources are titled, *Plagiarism Defined in Easy to Understand Terms, Tips on How to Avoid Both Internet-based and Conventional Plagiarism,* and *Answers to Frequently Asked Questions, Including Explanations for Often Misunderstood Concepts Like Fair Use, Public Domain, and Copyright Laws.*

For Further Reading

Books

John Alderman, *Sonic Boom: Napster, MP3, and the New Pioneers of Music*. New York: Perseus Publishing, 2001. An expert cyberjournalist explores the cultural, ethical, and legal issues raised by file sharing via the Internet.

David Callahan, *The Cheating Culture: Why More Americans Are Doing Wrong to Get Ahead*. New York: Harcourt, 2004. A New York Times best seller that exposes the increase in cheating over the last two decades and offers suggestions for reversing the trend.

Mark Fainaru-Wada and Lance Williams, *Game of Shadows: Barry Bonds, BALCO, and the Steroids Scandal that Rocked Professional Sports*. New York: Gotham Books, 2006. The riveting story of Barry Bonds and Bay Area Lab Co-operative (BALCO) that supplied banned drugs to professional athletes—told by the award-winning reporters who broke the news.

Randolph M. Feezell, *Sport, Play, and Ethical Reflection*. Urbana: University of Illinois Press, 2004. Chock-full of examples, this book explores the relationship between the serious and playful nature of competitive sports. It addresses cheating, ethics, and character building.

Blaine J. Fowers, *Beyond the Myth of Marital Happiness: How Embracing Virtues of Loyalty, Generosity, Justice, and Courage Can Strengthen Your Relationship*. San Francisco: Jossey-Bass, 2000. This counseling psychologist holds that happy, loyal, and long-lasting marriages are still possible in a cheating society if couples focus on partnership, friendship, and generosity.

Harry Frankfurt, *On Bullshit*. Princeton, NJ: Princeton University Press, 2005. Written by one of the world's foremost moral philosophers, the author uses humor and logic to address the difference between bullshitters—people who want to appear differently from whom they are—and outright liars.

Stuart P. Green, *Lying, Cheating, and Stealing: A Moral Theory of White-*

Collar Crime. New York: Oxford University Press, 2006. Motivated by the recent slew of corporate scandals, this book delves in the grey area of the law where normal business practices are not always legal.

Kathryn Jay, *More Than Just a Game: Sports in American Life Since 1945*. New York: Columbia University Press, 2004. A fascinating 60-year overview of professional sports and the complex forces responsible for creating the winning-cheating strategy that has become so popular.

Ann Lathrop and Kathleen Foss, *Guiding Students from Cheating and Plagiarism to Honesty and Integrity: Strategies for Change*. Westport, CT: Libraries Unlimited, 2005. A practical guide to changing school culture from one that tolerates cheating by students to one that promotes honesty and accountability.

Steven Levitt and Stephen Dubner, *Freakonomics: A Rogue Economist Explores the Hidden Side of Everything*. New York: William Morrow, 2005. A fun to read analysis of cheating and crime with a juxtaposition of topics such as a comparison of schoolteachers and sumo wrestlers.

Charles Lewis, *The Cheating of America: How Tax Avoidance and Evasion by the Super Rich Are Costing the Country Billions and What You Can Do About It*. New York: William Morrow, 2001. This book sets out to prove that the super-rich are at the root of the multi-billion dollar tax gap and offers a solution.

Robert F. Pace, *Halls of Honor: College Men in the Old South*. Baton Rogue: Louisiana State University Press, 2004. An anecdotal account of the "student peer-developed honor ethic" that transitions students from childhood to adulthood.

Pepper Schwartz and Dominic Cappello, *Ten Talks Parents Must Have with Their Children about Sex and Characte.*, New York: Hyperion, 2000. A guidebook exploring healthy teen relationships based on the concepts of boundaries, trust, and commitment.

Jeffrey Seglin, *The Right Thing: Conscience, Profit and Personal Responsibility in Today's Business*. Rollinsford, NH: Spiro Press, 2003. A compilation of Seglin's *New York Times* business columns on ethics and the power of leading by example.

William N. Taylor, *Anabolic Steroids and the Athlete*. Jefferson, NC: McFarland , 2002. A comprehensive look at anabolic steroids including the risks versus rewards, the principles of muscle building, medical uses, and addictions.

Joe Williams, *Cheating Our Kids: How Politics and Greed Ruin Education.* New York: Palgrave Macmillian, 2005. An investigation of the negative impact that politics and special interest groups are having on American public education and a strategy for parents to combat it.

Bernard E. Whitley Jr. and Patricia Keith-Spiegel, *Academic Dishonesty: An Educator's Guide.* Mahwah, NJ: Lawrence Erlbaum, 2002. The authors define and examine the prevalence of academic cheating and provide strategies to counteract, confront, and correct the problem while fostering a culture of integrity.

Periodicals

Gerard Baker, "Five Years After Enron, Culture of Greed Is Back," *Times (United Kingdom),* June 20, 2006.

Christine Brennan, "Get a Grip: Not All Baseball Cheating Is Created Equal," *USA Today,* October 24, 2006.

Les T. Csorba, "The Death of Character," *Boston Globe,* December 22, 2004.

Barbara Ehrenreich, "A Storm of Greed," *Progressive,* January 2006.

Jennifer Floyd Engel, "Cheaters Suddenly Prosper," *Fort Worth Star-Telegram,* January 7, 2007.

Adriana Ermter, "His Cheating Heart," *Flare,* May 2005.

Adrian Florido, "Cheating Definition Questioned: Administrators and Students Disagree About What Actions Constitute Cheating," *Daily Trojan,* March 9, 2006.

Fort Worth Star-Telegram, "It's Stealing, and It's All the Same," June 15, 2006.

Stephen Gandel "EZ Does It," *Money,* April 2006.

Jonathan D. Glater, "Cheating Gets Easier with Gadgetry," *New York Times,* May 18, 2006.

Pedro Ruz Gutierrez, "False Returns, True Crimes," *Orlando Sentinel,* April 14, 2005.

Monica Hatcher, "On Website, Women Identify Cheaters," *Miami Herald,* September 28, 2005.

Dana Hudepohl, "Everything You Know About Affairs Is Wrong," *Redbook,* May 2006.

Philip Johnson, "Cheating: Are We Part of the Problem?" *The Teaching Professor*, April 2005.

Tim Logan, "Schumer Wants Cheaters to Pay," *Times Herald-Record*, August 4, 2006.

Jonathan Malesic, "How Dumb Do They Think We Are," *Chronicle of Higher Education*, December 15, 2006.

Kymm Mann, "In Digital Age, Answers at Fingertip," *Appeal-Democrat*, May 7, 2007.

Kathleen Kennedy Manzo, "Houston Inspector Finds Cheating on State Tests," *Education Week*, May 18, 2005.

Robert S. McIntyre, "Reducing the Tax Gap," *FDCH Congressional Testimony*, January 23, 2007.

Stephen Moore, "Supply Side: Those April Blues," *Wall Street Journal*, April 23, 2007.

Rick Morrissey, "Sometimes College Coaches Just Can't Win," *Chicago Tribune*, February 8, 2007.

David J. Neal, "Cheating Pays Off for Chargers' Merriman," *Miami Herald*, December 19, 2006.

David Shaw, "Ethical Journalists? Hey, It Turns Out We Really Are," *Los Angeles Times*, February 13, 2005.

Lisa Smell, "How Schools Cheat," *Reason*, June 2005.

Jack Z. Smith, "An Honest Effort Could Reap Billions," *Fort Worth Star-Telegram*, March 16, 2007.

Teen People, "Confessions," September 2006.

Matthew S. Willen, "Reflections on the Cultural Climate of Plagiarism," *Liberal Education*, Fall 2004.

Mike Zimmerman, "Monogamy Rules," *Men's Health*, October 2005.

Index

Picture Credits

Cover: photos.com
All photos © AP Images